WIPF & STOCK · Eugene, Oregon

WHAT'S GOD UP TO ON PLANET EARTH?
A No-Strings Attached Explanation of the Christian Message.

Copyright © 2011 Mark Keown. All rights reserved. Except for brief quotations in critical publications or reviews, no part of this book may be reproduced in any manner without prior written permission from the publisher. Write: Permissions, Wipf and Stock Publishers, 199 W. 8th Ave., Eugene, OR 97401.

Wipf & Stock
An imprint of Wipf and Stock Publishers
199 W. 8th Avenue, Suite 3
Eugene OR, 97401
www.wipfandstock.com

ISBN 13: 978-1-61097-132-4

Manufactured in the U.S.A.

Editing & Typesetting:
Andrew Killick
Castle Publishing Services

Design:
Jeff Tebbutt & Lydia Parker
Roll Creative

All scriptures are taken from the HOLY BIBLE,
NEW INTERNATIONAL VERSION®. NIV®.
Copyright© 1973, 1978, 1984 by International Bible Society.
Used by permission of Zondervan. All rights reserved.

FOREWORD

People have mixed feelings about the Christian faith – some are indifferent to it, some are actively hostile to it, and some view it as an artefact of history.

But it is also an undeniable fact that, all the time, there are people moving towards and embracing Christianity. Sometimes suddenly, often gradually, they experience a significant change in their lives, accompanied by major shifts in their beliefs, attitudes and values.

These people appear to discover that Christianity makes sense of life, death, relationships, work and pleasure. God becomes the anchoring point of their whole lives. Instead of that gnawing sense that life in this vast universe is ultimately pointless, they find purpose and meaning, and a growing personal wholeness.

One famous twentieth century author and scholar – a man who fiercely resisted faith, then became a convinced believer – was Professor C.S. Lewis. He wrote: 'Christianity, if false, is of no importance, and if true, of infinite importance.' The implication is that if there is any possibility that Christianity and the Bible are true, then we should investigate them.

Mark Keown has written this book for that purpose – to aid in our investigation of the Christian faith and to gain a better understanding of what we believe.

What's God up to on Planet Earth? is not superficial. It is undergirded by scholarship, but not too technical. It is written from the heart. It is honest and balanced. It focuses on the central issues, and does not get sidetracked.

Dr Keown is well qualified to write this book – he himself was once indifferent to God, but is now passionate about the Christian faith, a lively and clear communicator, and a credible scholar. He lives by what he believes. I warmly commend this book.

Dr Stuart Lange (Laidlaw College)

CONTENTS

Acknowledgements	9
Introduction	11
1. Relationship	15
2. Rupture	31
3. Restoration	47
4. Return	73
5. Response	91
6. Where to from here?	109
Appendices:	
Am I Really a Sinner?	121
Other Resources	128
Notes	138
About the Author	160

ACKNOWLEDGEMENTS

Thanks to my wonderful wife Emma, the most extraordinary woman in the world. Keep preaching it! Thanks to my three super daughters Gracie, Annie and Esther, I hope and pray you live this out until the end. You light up my world.

Thanks to all those who have allowed me to test this material out especially the people of St Columba Presbyterian, Greenlane Presbyterian, Mt Roskill Baptist and Glenfield Presbyterian churches. Thanks to the staff and students of Laidlaw College. Special thanks to Brian Chitty who led me to Christ and to Sean Pawson who taught me the gospel; you did well. I am forever indebted to you both.

Thanks to all those who have helped in different ways with this project: Craig Blomberg, Gerald Bray, Naomi Quirke, Stuart Lange, Adrienne Hunt, Emma Keown, Gracie Keown, Annie Keown, Martyn Newbie, George Dunning, Angelene Goodman, Neil Walker and Julian and Claire Doorey. To Jeff Tebbutt and Lydia Parker who designed the cover, I deeply appreciate your hard work and vision. A special thanks to Andrew Killick for your guidance, editing and over-sight of the final product.

Thanks most especially to the one whose story this is, God, Father, Son and Spirit. I hope and pray you are pleased with this and use it for your glory.

INTRODUCTION

Hi, I'm Mark Keown, and this book was written to help you get a handle on the Christian faith. It's designed as a 'no-strings-attached' presentation of what is commonly called the Christian gospel, or 'the good news'. It's intended to give an intelligent and coherent explanation of what God is up to in this world with a particular emphasis on us human beings.

The book is 'no-strings-attached' in the sense that its purpose is not to enlist you in a particular church, get money from you or tell you what to believe. Instead, you can take it home, read it, process it and decide for yourself what you think about it. I would be lying if I didn't admit to hoping that you, like me, would find yourself believing the message and want to follow Jesus. However, this book is written so that you can consider the message yourself, without a preacher or church hassling you. You can take it or leave it.

I became a Christian in 1985 at the age of 24. I didn't grow up in a 'Christian' home but first remember hearing the Christian message as a teenager while living in the Cook Islands. I found the message convincing but didn't become involved in Christianity until I left home and came face to face with the challenges of life. I became disillusioned with the greed and futility of much of our western society. On one level our civilisation is impressive with its wealth, technology and science, but I couldn't escape my feelings of deep spiritual emptiness, not to mention my concern at a growing loss of morality that threatened to destroy me and the fabric of our society. I became concerned that unless there was some intervention or transformation, the western world was heading for a terrible crisis.

I also had a series of spiritual experiences that led me to convert to Christianity. Without any additional intervention by Christians, I decided to buy a Bible, began to read it and went to church. In that process I came face to face with the shocking realisation that there is a God, that Jesus is not a lunatic, a liar, a legend or a deluded false Messiah, but is the Lord, and that I could know him personally. I found a whole lot of other people who had found this same Jesus and I could see that while they were human like you and me with their faults, they had a love, hope and optimism that impressed me. While still flawed, they had a power in their lives that could change them inwardly – a power that I wanted too. I saw Christian families that stunned me with their love for each other. I discovered true love in the communities where they gathered. So I gave my life to Jesus and joined the church and since then I have never left or wanted to leave, despite sometimes finding church life a bit of a challenge.

God has changed me. With his help I turned away from addiction to alcohol, shallow pleasure and a desire for personal glory through sport. I've gone from university dropout to a pastor and a doctor, and lecturer in theology. As I've studied the faith, my belief has matured into an intellectual and emotional confidence that the Christian message is true. God has changed my life and my perspective, and for that I am eternally grateful.

I write this book hoping that, as you read it, you too will become gripped by what God is really up to on planet earth. No doubt you will already have a few ideas about Christianity and may have had negative experiences of Christians and the Church. I don't want you to forget about or trivialise those experiences, but I ask you to set them aside for a moment and read this book with an open mind. I want to apologise on behalf of the Christians who have let you, and others, down over the last 2000 years. Throughout history, a lot of things have been done in the name of Jesus that were not the kinds of things that Jesus would have done. We Christians are not 'better' than other people. I hope you will realise that while Christians and the Church have made mistakes, this does not invalidate the message of Jesus himself who, as this book will show, is the centre and end of everything.

In this book, I crystallise the Christian message into five easy to understand and remember words, and then develop the concepts behind them. I call these the 5 R's of the Gospel (the Christian message). This is your opportunity to consider the merits of the message and where you stand in relation to them and to God. Not all your questions will be answered here, so I have included endnotes that refer to Bible verses or passages. Some of the endnotes suggest different views and ideas that Christians hold on various things. There is also an appendix which will point you to other books that may answer your questions. If you want to check out what I have written, it may be helpful to have a Bible handy and look at the verses as you go. So let's begin…

ONE
RELATIONSHIP

In this chapter we will discuss God's original plan. It's the story of a glorious cosmic project in which God created humanity to have a relationship with him in an awe-inspiring world. It will give an answer to the question, 'Why am I here?'

God

The starting point for the Christian faith is God himself. Christianity is based on God's existence. While most people from history and in the world today believe in a God or gods, the existence of divine beings is disputed by some (especially in the west). Atheists deny that there is a God. Others are agnostics, unsure whether there is a God or that he[1] can be known. It is possible that you are one of these people. In this book, I'm not going to seek to philosophically defend or prove God's existence.[2] In fact, I would agree with those who state that God cannot be *proved*. However, I suggest that a number of factors combine to suggest that belief in God is reasonable and compelling.

First, existence itself indicates a starting point of some sort with a glorious intelligence and power behind the formation of this world.[3] Secondly, the order we see in creation which science reveals, from the human cell to the far reaches of space, suggests that creation is not random and that there is a creative force behind it and at work in it.[4] Thirdly, the common sense of morality and goodness that is found across human societies suggests the possibility of a God.[5] Finally, for me, it is the flow of history and especially the historical person Jesus who brings me to the view that there is a God and that Jesus reveals him to us.

The sweep of the Bible story from creation, to Jesus, to a new creation, is set in the context of the real history of ancient empires, people, places and societies. The 66 books found in the Bible are remarkably coherent with fulfilled predictions, a real account of existence, and a future hope for a fallen world. As I have come to believe in God, despite great doubts, and have accepted Jesus, I too have tangibly experienced his 'presence' in my life. All these factors combine to cause me to believe in God and believe that Christ is the supreme revelation of who God is. I hope that whether you are an atheist, an agnostic or a believer in another religious viewpoint, that you will read on and give this message a chance. I pray and believe that as you do, you will be drawn to God and his love.

The Bible starts with the words 'in the beginning God'![6] Genesis 1:1 points to a dimension that existed prior to the existence of our world, in which God existed. We call this home of God 'heaven'. By looking at Scripture (the Bible) and the world, we can identify at least five attributes that are critical to understanding why he created in the first place: he is all powerful, creative, loving, eternal and pure.[7] Let's look at these concepts one at a time.

First, God is *all powerful*. The technical word for this is 'omnipotent'. This means he can do all things except what is 'absurd' or is contradictory to his character. As the ancient Hebrew thinker Job put it, 'I know you (God) can do all things.'[8] God is a super being who is capable of extraordinary and unimaginable acts. This universe with its astonishing glory demonstrates that.

Secondly, God is unimaginably *creative* – that is, he is a creator.[9] At his heart God is clearly a being who loves to design and make stuff – and he is brilliant at doing so! You can see this in the complexity and glory of the universe.[10] God is the supreme artist, scientist and musician who has complete command of every artistic and scientific field. Our own art, science, music, and any other creativity, confined as it is to our experience of God's created order and the minds he has given us, merely reflect the brilliance seen in his world. This world is a product of his awe-inspiring genius and he cares about every part of it wanting it all to reflect his being in its brilliance and goodness.

Thirdly, God is *loving* – or, as one of Jesus' first followers and best friends John put it, 'God is love'.[11] The love we are talking about here is not romantic, sentimental, mushy or sexual love. Rather, it is a love that is characterised by compassion-motivated actions on behalf of others – a love that serves and gives. Indeed, 'love' in the Bible is really a verb – it is an attitude that leads to action. As such, God is loving by nature and all he does comes from a desire to love and to see love spread. He is relational (i.e. relationships are important to him), yearning from his being to love and to enjoy being freely loved in return.

Fourthly, God is *eternal*. This means he exists before time, through time and beyond time. Those who study the Bible describe him as 'omnipresent', meaning he exists at all points of time in all of his creation simultaneously. The notion of God being eternal is introduced in the first book of the Bible: 'Abraham planted a tamarisk tree in Beersheba, and there he called upon the name of the Lord, the *Eternal* God.'[12] Later in the Bible, Paul says of God, 'now to the King *eternal*, immortal, invisible, the only God, be honour and glory for ever and ever. Amen!'[13] His eternal nature is important in that he also wants to grant 'eternal life' to every human who has and ever will live.[14] His intention is to live forever with us.

Finally, God is *pure*.[15] That is, God is 'too pure to look upon evil'; he 'cannot tolerate wrong.'[16] Put another way, he is 'not a God who takes pleasure in evil', and with him 'the wicked cannot dwell'.[17] Another way of saying this is that God is 'holy', meaning that he is without evil and so will not ultimately accept evil in any form. In a sense we can say that God is allergic to evil – he is too pure to live in its presence. Another simple way of putting this is to say that God is entirely good.

This concept is important because it is the basis of God's justice, whereby he will eventually permanently destroy evil. It also helps us see God's gracious love and patience in the present as he tolerates the existence of evil in this time of human existence, despite it being utterly abhorrent to him. Furthermore, it points to the nature of heaven – a dimension in which God exists, and which is totally without evil and in which evil cannot exist.[18] As a consequence, no being that is evil in any way can dwell within its bounds in relationship with God. This means that if ever humanity fell into impurity, their relationship with God would be ruptured and they would be separated from him.

Creation

So, this loving, relational, eternal creator designed and made our world. The account of creation in the first book of the Bible Genesis tells us that God established the universe and our world with its sun and moon as a perfectly fine-tuned environment in which life could be formed. He created vegetation and animals to inhabit and populate the world. He created humanity as the climax of his creation. Indeed, the whole narrative of creation in the first two chapters of Genesis climaxes in the creation of humanity – creation is for us.

As you are no doubt aware, the exact method and process of this creation is an area of great controversy from the perspectives of science and faith.[19] This is not the place for an extensive discussion of the matter.

However, a few comments are important. Modern science assumes an old earth (approx. 4.5 billion years) and universe (approx. 13-14 billion years), and an evolutionary perspective of biological development. Some, usually more conservative Christians, reject this entirely and argue for a literal six-day event and a very young earth (less than 20,000 years old). Other Christians accept an old universe and earth, but reject the notion of evolutionary development, seeing the development of human life as sudden rather than a process (called 'old earth creationism'). Yet others prefer the notion of 'intelligent design' which is a broad notion that takes in a wide range of views, but is united in its belief that the complexity of the world as we know it requires an external force or power to exist. A growing number of Christians are now accepting the premises of science but arguing that evolutionary development and creation are not irreconcilable ('evolutionary theism' or 'theistic evolution').

The important thing to realise is that, contrary to popular thinking, Christians are not all anti-science and evolution. Indeed, many would argue that creation and science are not mutually exclusive. It is also important to note that many of history's greatest scientific minds, including Blaise Pascal, Isaac Newton and today, John Polkinghorne, based their thinking on the existence of God.

Whichever interpretation of creation in the first two chapters of Genesis Christians hold, all agree with the premise that God created the world. If you personally hold an evolutionary perspective, I encourage you to continue to read on as what you will read here does not depend on any particular view of creation. That is, it is possible to believe in God and still accept many of the views of modern science.[20]

Returning to our main point... The reason God created humanity is so that they could have a loving relationship with him and with each other in the world he created. He made humanity, male and female, in his own image.[21] Being made in the image of God means that each of us is made to be in some way *like God* (without being God or gods). We are made to be people of creativity and love. That is, we humans are created to be completely whole in our own skins and ready for relationship – a relationship with our creator, with each other, and with creation itself.[22] He granted humanity sovereignty or the power to rule over all of his creation. This means he has given people a responsibility to both use the natural world and to care for it deeply as human society develops. He is greatly concerned about every part of his world and, as his image bearers charged with caring for it, so should we. God's project involves us working with him and under his reign. We are to build God's world.

Relationship with God

Firstly and primarily, we humans were made to have a *relationship with God* himself. The first basic truth of the gospel from an individual personal point of view is that 'God made me to have a relationship with him'. This relationship is, in many ways, like human interpersonal relationships, but in other ways it is different. It is the relationship of the Creator with the created, the infinite with the finite, the immortal with the mortal. Because of this, we need to take care at this point to define this relationship appropriately.

The nature of the relationship between God and humanity was always intended to be two-sided. From God's point of view, he wants to use his immense power to love each person, bless them, lead them, guide them, provide for them, protect them, nurture them and walk through life with them. Put another way, he wants to 'hang out' with us. He wants to be our friend, knowing us, caring for us and enjoying our company.

This is seen in the account of the Garden of Eden where he provided humanity with the beauty and perfection of the Garden and walked with them in the shade of the trees.[23] He wants this relationship to be everlasting. In other words, he wants to spend eternity with you and me. In the movie *Bruce Almighty*[24] there is a scene in which God (Morgan Freeman) chats to Bruce (Jim Carrey) as they mop the floor, working together, enjoying each other's company. Or think of a parent spending time with their child maybe fishing or shopping together; God wants to spend time with us.

This desire is symbolised in the story of Genesis 2-3 by the tree of life in the centre of the garden, the fruit of which would give Adam and Eve eternal life.[25] The first humans were able to eat of it at any time. It would enable them to live eternally and be sustained in their relationship with God.[26]

Effectively this was an invitation to join God who is triune (three, yet one) – Father, Son and Spirit. The concept of the Trinity states that God is eternally One in being, yet exists in three eternal simultaneous forms; One yet three – three yet One. We are not a hundred percent sure how this works. I mean, who can work out the notion of a cosmic eternal being who is one and also existing in three forms simultaneously? But it seems from the Bible that God is supreme, is one in character, psyche, connectedness, essence and community, yet exists in three totally unified and intimately connected individual personal beings.[27]

Hence, the Christian God is different from the Muslim God who is one in a literal mathematical sense, removing any notion of his becoming human. The Muslim God then is a 'distant' God who is difficult to relate to. The Christian God is also different to the many Hindu gods who are totally present, distinct, a blend of good and evil and who are supposedly with us in many forms and ways. The Christian God is one but exists in three perfectly united, good, connected, pure modes; all with different functions but on perfectly equal terms, utterly one but expressed in three (the Godhead). He is beyond us in glory (transcendent), yet present with us in history (immanent).

At his heart, this God is one in unity – that is, a unity of community. Hence, our invitation to accept the Christian message is not only an invitation to join God, but also an invitation to join the community of God's being[28] and the wider heavenly community.[29] Consequently, a person who enters into a relationship with God joins the triune God and the many heavenly beings in a community of love. We don't become God or gods, but we enter into a deep and intimate spiritual relationship with God and his people. The unity of the Godhead is the ideal for community, the three eternal persons of God being one in love and purpose and living in perfect harmony and peace. Heaven, as it exists now, is similarly a place of purity and unity which God will preserve at all costs. In a sense then, the communities of believers that exist on earth are meant to be extensions of the heavenly community – colonies of heaven on earth that demonstrate and extend the heavenly community.[30]

The best way to understand God in these terms is through the human experience of parenting. God is often called 'Father'. This is an English translation taken from the intimate Aramaic family term of endearment used by Jesus and Paul to refer to God in the New Testament (*Abba*).[31] As 'Father', God embodies the fullness of the ideal of human parenting, including in his being the notions of motherhood and fatherhood.[32] Just as a young couple want to create a child to love, nurture, provide for, protect and guide through life, God is the cosmic parent of us all, who created with a desire to have a relationship with us.

Ideally each person will walk in a flawless, direct and open relationship with God. He or she would know God and be his friend, experiencing his blessing and returning trust, gratitude and love. However, we are not equals with God, so our relationship with him is also one of the created to the creator; the limited to the all-powerful, the mortal to the immortal, the finite to the infinite. The only right response of humanity to such an awesome being is awe, reverence, gratitude, obedience, humility, allegiance and service.

Another way of putting it is that every human was created *to worship God*.[33] This isn't just something that happens at church, but is an ongoing life attitude, serving God, accepting his offer of love and taking our place in caring for and developing the world. It needs to be pointed out that, from God's point of view, this is not a relationship of domination. He does not seek to force us into submission. He will cherish us and dote over us as a mother over her newborn child. We should live lives of gratitude, placing him above everything else and glorifying him.

When Jesus was asked which of the ten commandments was the most important, he said, 'Love the Lord your God with all your heart, with all your soul, with all your mind, and with all your strength.'[34] Every human was created to be loved by God and to love God. Humans are the children in a cosmic parent-child relationship. We are created to be children of God, loving our divine Father, walking in relationship with him.[35]

Relationship with Each Other

Humanity was not created only to love God. Secondly, and equally fundamentally, we were created to express the love placed in us by God to one another. God formed Eve from Adam and they became one (marriage) and had children. The family based upon a harmonious marriage between a man and a woman is the basic unit of human society. In its ideal form, it embodies the concept that humanity can live in harmony, loving, respecting and honouring one another with the same love God has for each person.[36] Consequently, Jesus said that the second greatest commandment is to 'love your neighbour as yourself.'[37] A deep examination of the teaching of the Bible indicates that love for God and for each other is thoroughly intertwined.[38] That is, a failure to love others is in effect a failure to love God, in whose image we are made.[39]

Returning to our father-child analogy, we are created to be a family, loving each other across all humanity. God's ideal is that we both love him and one another. This does not mean a blurring of individual distinctiveness; it is a unity in diversity. Each of us is unique and born to express our own being and brilliance in a totally unique way. But God's vision is that we do so in love and unity, one people without war or division at any level.

Relationship with Creation and the World

A third dimension of relationship is found in the story of creation. Humanity was given the charge of caring for creation itself.[40] The world that humanity has been given is to be carefully managed to retain ecological balance. We have been given the world to explore its splendour and glory and to use what we find with the creativity that is granted us, for human good. However, we must also show great care and concern for the natural world including the flora and fauna. God is concerned for every living thing, every tree, the animal world and every part of this creation. Hence, we should be deeply concerned at the current ecological problems and in particular, the disintegration of the environment, irrespective of its causes.

God's hope for planet earth is that it will be a world of love and harmony, where people will live together in perfect love for God and one another, utilising the resources and caring for the world as people express their creativity in work and play. God cares for the whole of the world and his original intention is that human society would be full of goodness and love. So as people spread out and formed society, it was God's desire that it be wonderfully creative and unified as it richly expressed its God-given creativity. We should value every part of human life. God cares about the arts, the sciences, sport, economics, family, governments, music, literature, ecology and life itself.

Each one of us is created by God (through the natural processes of human reproduction) with a purpose. Each of us is born with a unique set of talents to express our humanity. Each of us has a brilliance to be realised in relationship with God in and for this world and its people. Through this uniqueness, together we will build God's world and bring into being God's great dream and project.

Relationship with Self

Although not explicitly stated in the text, it is implied that the first humans were completely comfortable in themselves. There was no self-hate, lack of self-esteem, guilt, shame, depression, anxiety or personal angst. This is seen in their lack of shame.[41] The first created humans were at total peace; their private worlds were in order and harmony. They were comfortable with who they were physically, intellectually, spiritually and emotionally. They did not experience jealousy or other desires which stem from a shattered inner being. They were whole and unbroken without the problems that blight us in this troubled world.

Freedom

There is another aspect of love that is an important part of the Christian message – the concept of freedom or volition. Initially humanity in the Garden was free. They were free to live there, work, enjoy it and be nourished by its produce. They could eat of the tree of life which would sustain them, meaning that this life of peace would be eternal; living forever with God and each other in God's sensational world. However, they were innocently unaware of their freedom, not knowing anything other than the perfection in which they lived.

This is where the story gets a little more complex. If love is to be recognised and experienced as love, it requires not only the giving of freedom but the gaining of the knowledge or recognition of one's freedom – the freedom to accept or reject love. This being so, God did not create humans as automatons or robots who would simply return his love without choice. Rather, he created humans in his image to have freedom and the ability to accept or reject him. His desire is for a genuine relationship with each and every human being in the world.

God enabled this awareness of freedom by first creating relational people with intelligence, creativity, emotions and discernment. He then placed them in a garden of perfection,[42] full of the most wonderful food to eat and which they were to care for and enjoy.[43] The first humans were utterly free and innocent within the constraints of the garden, but did not fully comprehend it as they were not aware of any alternative.

God made them aware of their *freedom* in two interconnected ways. First, he did so with a prohibition against eating from one tree in particular – the tree of the knowledge of good and evil.[44] The introduction of this command created a boundary which the humans could not cross without suffering the consequences.[45]

Secondly, along with that prohibition, he allowed into the garden a spiritual antagonist who had already abused the freedom given by God's love. This enemy is known as Satan and he is symbolised as a snake in the story of Genesis.[46] This implies that Satan (or the devil) and his minions had at some previous stage violated their relationship with God and had suffered the consequence of being banished from God's presence.[47] In the garden, Satan twisted God's words and used them to seduce Eve and Adam (the first humans) to respond to their own desire and eat the fruit of the tree of knowledge of good and evil – thereby disobey God (this is examined further in chapter two).[48] The combination of prohibition and Satan's distortion provided the choice which the true knowledge of freedom requires.

In addition, the existence of Satan introduced the potential for utter evil to be released into the cosmos and, as such, made humanity aware of the distinction between good and evil. Good can exist without evil, but cannot be discerned as good unless the recipients are aware of the antithesis of good. Without the existence of Satan and evil, choice would not be genuine and knowledge of freedom would not exist. As such 'the Fall' (see chapter two), while very much a cosmic disaster, had a kind of positive spin-off for the purposes of God's work on earth.

People would, in essence, become like Truman in the movie *The Truman Show*.[49] Truman lived in a perfect world unaware that anything existed beyond the world created for him by Christoph and hence, not free or aware of the absence of true freedom. When an object fell from the sky and interrupted his seemingly perfect world, this set off a chain of events that made Truman aware that the world was not all he thought it was. He then became aware of his lack of freedom, and chose to leave the world created for him – he exercised this freedom to walk away. The difference between *The Truman Show* and our world is that Truman gained his freedom when he took the choice given him; whereas humanity lost their freedom when they took the choice given by God. As a result, we face death and a dreadful deterioration in our circumstances.

Thus God, in his great love, gave humanity choice (or 'free will') and with it the freedom to make a decision to love freely. Humans are volitional beings created by God with the capacity to accept or reject love. God's purpose now is to win them over by his mercy, grace and beneficence.

Referring back to our parenting analogy, God is the ideal cosmic parent who, after providing everything his children would ever need, is prepared to release them to experience life and make their own choices. Just as parenting involves risk – including the risk of rejection, of rebellion, of children going off the rails – so there is an inherent 'risk'[50] in God's actions. There was a possibility that some of his free people would turn against him. Yet, just as human parents are prepared to have children despite this risk, so God was prepared to create us. He believes in the power of love to overcome. He was willing to create us because, although many would turn away from him, he believed that it was worth it for those who would say yes.[51]

Conclusion

To summarise then, the starting point for the gospel is 'relationship'. We are each made to have a relationship with God. As an old saying common in Christian circles goes, 'within each human heart is a God-shaped vacuum' that can only be filled with God's presence. Christianity is not a set of rules, it is not a religion of ritual and 'do's and do not's', 'should's and should not's' – it is a relationship. It is a relationship between a cosmic eternal personal being of love and creativity and his created, volitional beings. As part of that relationship we will live out our uniqueness with our special abilities to see God's world become what he dreams it to be.

So the great question, 'Why am I here?' from a Christian point of view finds its answer in the concept of relationship. We are created to love as God has loved us – loving him, loving one another and loving the creation given to us. As we do this, each in our own unique way, we will build God's world as he intended. In terms of our overall question, 'What's God up to on planet earth?', he has created humanity for an eternal loving relationship with him. He has created humanity to express their individuality in unity, in partnership with God, co-creating with him to build his glorious world.

But this is just the beginning of our journey. As we will see in the next chapter, the original intention of God has been violated and this has had some far-reaching consequences…

Questions for Reflection

1. Is there a God or gods? Is there any evidence? Consider alternative explanations for reality.
2. What is your journey of believing or not believing? Perhaps write it down and reflect on it.
3. If there is a God? What is he like? How might we describe God?
4. Do you agree that love and relationship lies at the heart of existence?
5. How do you think the first three chapters of Genesis should be read? Literally? Symbolic/literal? Myth?
6. What is the place of freedom and volition? Is it essential to love? Are humans truly free? What is freedom?
7. How do you see yourself? Do you have a sense of worth? Does the existence of a God who 'loves you as you are' change things for you?

TWO
RUPTURE

In chapter one we discussed the idea that humanity was created by God for a love-based relationship with the creator of the universe, with each other and with the world. This chapter introduces the second R of the Christian message, 'Rupture'. Here we will discuss how God's plan has been disrupted. We will find that, just as a cataclysmic earthquake splits the earth, so the relationships between God and his created people, between people themselves, and between humankind and the world itself have been torn apart and are in need of restoration.

Most people recognise intuitively that things are not what they could be, so here we will discuss how the Bible explains the problem. If chapter one answered the question 'Why am I here?' This chapter answers the question, 'What's wrong with the world?'

The Fall

The 'Rupture' refers to the rupturing of the intended relationship between God, humanity and the world. This came about at what Christians call 'the fall of humankind' (or 'the Fall').[1]

After God prohibited Adam and Eve (the first humans) from eating the fruit of the tree of the knowledge of good and evil in the Garden of Eden, the snake (Satan),[2] enticed Adam and Eve to eat the forbidden fruit. He came to Eve and asked her a simple question: 'Did God *really* say, "you must not eat from any tree in the garden?"' Eve responded by misquoting God, failing to recall his words accurately: 'We may eat fruit from the trees in the garden, but God did say, "You must not eat fruit from the tree that is in the middle of the garden, and you must not *touch* it, or you will die".' This was a distortion and an amplification of God's words. He had said 'do not *eat* it'; she reported that he said 'do not *touch* it'.[3]

Then the snake responded, 'You will not surely die, for God knows that when you eat of it your eyes will be opened, and you will be like God, knowing good and evil.'[4] This involved an out and out lie followed by a half-truth. The lie was suggesting that 'you will not surely die' which directly contradicted God's explicit warning.[5] The half-truth was that their eyes would be opened and they would be like God, knowing good and evil. That their eyes would be opened was true in a sense – like God, they would realise the difference between good and evil. However, in other ways they would be less like God. They would be separated from him and they would no longer be a pure reflection of his image. They would no longer be sustained by the tree of life and the image of God in humanity would be damaged. Unlike God, they would no longer be good. Neither would they be anything like God in power, as he alone is all-powerful.

The story says that Eve, seduced not only by the attractiveness of the fruit and its apparent gourmet qualities, was also drawn in by Satan's words that it would make her like God. She interpreted this as meaning that she would have the wisdom of God, and she ate the fruit. She then gave some to her husband who *was with her at the time* and he too ate it.[6] Adam's presence mentioned here indicates that while Eve took the initiative, Adam was equally culpable of disobedience ('sin'). As a result, their relationship with God was ruptured.[7]

As soon as they had eaten, all 'hell' broke loose. First, *their relationship with their inner self was shattered*. Instantly they realised they were naked and experienced shame, guilt and self-deprecation for the first time.[8] This outcome points to the initial shattering of self-esteem and the introduction of fear, guilt and shame into human experience. Psychologically, the image of God, while still intact to a degree, had been badly broken.

Secondly, *their relationship with God was fractured*. The story goes on to tell us that God came looking for them, so that he could walk with them in the garden in the cool of the day.[9] Imagine what that would have been like, to wander through a garden with the creator of the universe. But instead of finding his 'kids' happily playing in the garden, they were terrified because of their fear and shame when they heard him coming, and they hid (3:8).

So God called Adam, 'Where are you?' Adam was at least honest in responding, 'I heard you in the garden, and I was afraid because I was naked; so I hid.'[10] This revealed that they had sinned against God and the relationship between God and humanity was forever ruptured.

Why did such a seemingly small event lead to a rupture in the relationship? The answer is found in one particular attribute of God mentioned in chapter one – his perfect *purity* or *holiness*. God is pure and will not dwell with evil, unless it is dealt with, since it is repugnant to him. Hence, at the moment when humans disobeyed, rejected and rebelled against God, corruption was etched into human existence. Adam and Eve were the parents of all humanity and they passed this status down to their descendants through the ages.

Because of this, God was no longer able to dwell with humanity in this intimate, free relationship due to the impurity that violated his sense and being. He thus expelled Adam and Eve from the garden and barred them from having a direct relationship with him.[11] Access to the tree of life was also barred and so humanity became subject to death and decay.[12] If God had allowed them to remain in the garden and eat of the tree of life, they in their fallenness would have gained eternal existence and the universe would be forever blighted with the presence of evil.

The third consequence was that *their relationship with one another was ruptured*. When we read on we see that Adam and Eve instantly began to fight, seeking to blame someone else for their indiscretion.

First, Adam tried to blame Eve. When God asked them, 'Who told you that you were naked? Have you eaten from the tree that I commanded you not to eat from?'[13] Adam's response was to implicate Eve and, indirectly, God himself: 'The woman *you* put here with me – she gave me some fruit from the tree, and I ate it.'[14] Yet, as noted above, he was with her at the time of eating and was equally culpable. Here we have the first marital breakdown and family conflict. The basic unit of society was fractured. As many of us have experienced, human history has been dogged with broken families and human conflict at every level since that day. God's great dream of a world of harmony, love and unity was thus in great peril.

When God turned to the woman and asked her, 'What is this you have done?' She responded by blaming the snake: 'The serpent deceived me, and I ate.'[15] Again this is a typical human reaction and sounds like the murderer in the courtroom who says, 'The devil made me do it.'

A fourth consequence then was *the demise of God's great dream for his world*. God's dream is not just about individuals living in relationship with God and one another, but of humanity building God's world with all his creativity in love and harmony. It is a 'utopian' picture of all facets of existence including the arts, sciences, literature, music, sport and more, with each individual contributing in a unique way to building up

God's world; all of this in a place of unity, love, joy and peace. The Fall or Rupture shattered this. Each person became marred and flawed, unable to fully express their innate God-inspired brilliance because of their brokenness. Selfishness and personal ambition corrupted all humanity. Contention and domination became par for the course. God's world would now never be what God intended, unless it is restored.

The result of Adam and Eve's actions was the judgement of God on all. The snake was cursed to slide along the ground, probably meaning that he would contend on earth with humanity until ultimately defeated.[16] The woman was told that she would forever experience great pain in childbearing and live in constant conflict with man throughout human history and be subject to him. This represents the truth that patriarchy and family fragmentation will be a problem for all of time. This subjection is not God's ideal but a consequence of sin.[17]

The man was told he would spend his days slaving to produce food, contending with thorns and weeds. Finally he was told he would die, 'for dust you are and to dust you will return'.[18] Adam and Eve were banished from God's presence. Here we have humanity afflicted with pain and suffering, hunger and famine, conflict, contention with creation itself, separation from God and the introduction of our greatest enemy, death.

The Fall was a cosmic cataclysmic event affecting all of the created order. I sometimes imagine that as Eve and Adam ate that fruit in the garden, there was a sudden change in the weather, there was thunder and lightning, there were earthquakes and eruptions – the whole of the earth reacted to this terrible moment of disobedience. The world would never be as God intended it unless it could somehow be restored. Creation groaned as it was fragmented and subjected to decay.[19] Heaven itself was shaken in that moment.

All Corrupted by Sin

At the point of the Fall then, evil was let loose to affect God's creation. Corruption entered world history. Death, sickness, pain, war, and natural disasters were released. It was as if a virus was introduced into the cosmos, corrupting the whole earth – like a virulent strain of HIV, bird flu or Ebola infecting God's perfect creation; like a rot infecting a beautiful piece of fruit; like rust destroying iron… eating it away. No longer was creation 'very good' as God had first described it,[20] now – while it was still good in many ways – it was fatally flawed.

This corruption became part of the DNA of the whole living kingdom, death was released,[21] life was driven back, and the whole of the world became a war zone between life and death. The greatest manifestation of this 'disease' is that people say, 'I don't need God.' In so doing they deny their 'createdness' and the glory that stands behind the wonders of this world. Put another way, God has been usurped with the mantra, 'I am lord of my own destiny.' Every future descendent of Adam and Eve was corrupted from birth. Later in the Bible, King David said as much in the Psalms as he repented for taking Uriah's wife Bathsheba, committing adultery with her, and then sending Uriah to his death.[22] As an adulterer and a murderer he admits to God: 'surely I was sinful at birth, sinful from the time my mother conceived me.'[23] Even in his mother's womb he was corrupted. Solomon said the same when he consecrated the temple to God and prayed for the people: 'there is no one who does not sin.'[24] Jesus' words to the rich ruler, 'no one is good except God alone', imply the same.[25] The Apostle Paul speaks of universal human sinfulness when he says, 'Jews and Gentiles alike are *all* under sin … there is no one righteous, not even one… *all* have turned away… there is *no one* who does good, not even one: for *all* have sinned and fall short of the glory of God.'[26]

This all goes back to the Fall. Paul goes on to say, 'therefore, just as sin entered the world through one man [Adam], and death through sin, in this way death came to all people... *because* all sinned.'[27] The last clause is important because here Paul explains that death remains not just because of Adam and Eve; that would be unjust. Death remains because 'all sinned' – that is, we are all separated from God *because of our own individual sin*, not because of Adam and Eve. We are all prone to sin but we are also all responsible for it before God.

It is not that there is no good left in the world; after all, there obviously is! What is meant is that everything that exists is marred and no longer fully what God intended it to be. This applies to us individually. It also applies to human society, which is broken in every part. Human creativity, while remaining extraordinary, has become misguided – not concerned for human good and the careful management of the ecosystem but focussed on self-glorification and greed. Human society became stratified between the 'have's' and 'have not's'; between the powerful and the powerless. Racism, ageism, sexism, socio-economic inequality, war and other terrible inequalities are all a consequence of this essential corruption.

Creation itself has been marred by the influence of evil and corruption. Paul tells us that creation has been subjected to frustration, awaiting its liberation from bondage to decay. He uses the metaphor of creation groaning like a woman in labour as it yearns for release from the oppressions of evil.[28] Thus natural disasters may even be a result of this cataclysmic event.

The Real Problem: Evil

You may have heard Christians talking about the fact that sin is the main problem in the world, and in a sense it very much is. Sins are attitudes and behaviours that are contrary to God's ideals and goodness. Sin begins in the heart with attitudes and thoughts that violate goodness. Where behaviour is concerned, sin includes not only actions that actively violate God, other people, his world and ourselves, but also includes false attitudes and the failure to act when we should ('sins of omission'). That being said, while sin is a fair description of the human condition, the problem caused by the Fall goes a lot deeper than just human sin. The problem is in reality 'evil' – the antithesis of God who is 'Good'.

When God created the earth, it was 'very good'.[29] At the Fall, evil was let loose. As noted above, evil was permitted before the Fall in the person of Satan, in the physical form of a snake. However, until the Fall, Satan, while evil, was restrained, unable to directly infiltrate creation. Adam and Eve were in a perfect, innocent relationship with God. If they had remained in that state, they and creation could not have been distorted by evil. Satan however, was lurking, waiting and looking for his opportunity to corrupt humanity and creation, like a thief looking for an entry point.[30]

He got his opportunity when God forbade Adam and Eve from eating the fruit. Satan spoke to Eve and, through her misinterpretation of God's word, was able to seduce her to disobey God. At that moment, when they ate the fruit and God withdrew, Satan got his chance. He and his minions (demons, evil spirits) were let loose. He was able to find a foothold and began corrupting every dimension of the earth, distorting humanity and all of creation. This corruption is seen in natural disasters and death in the natural world. In humanity it is also seen in death, disease, pain, male dominance over women, racism, suffering, war, violence, oppression and greed leading to poverty.[31]

Satan has gained such a hold over the world that by the time of Christ, when Jesus went into the wilderness to face Satan, the devil was bold enough to offer him the kingdoms of the world if he would bow down to him.[32] Unlike Eve and Adam, who failed in the garden, Jesus resisted the temptation, refusing to bow down to Satan.

So the real problem God and humanity have to deal with is *evil*. At its heart, evil is found in the form of the person of Satan and his demons seeking to steal, kill and destroy God's world and humanity.[33] However, it would be wrong to blame Satan entirely. We humans are responsible for our own actions. Sin is seen in an individual way with each person doing wrong. It is reflected corporately in structures and institutions which are corrupted. One example is the Nazi movement in the mid-20th century. Sin here is structural and its influence is horrendous. Sin in all its individual and corporate forms is a microcosm of the macro problem of evil. It is evil expressed through fallen humanity.

Some people tend to use the word sin in a light and fluffy way. They can see the problem with extreme examples of evil such as the Holocaust, genocide or infanticide. But, they might ask, what is wrong with a few personal 'mistakes'? What's the big deal? But what is at stake here cannot be trivialised. When we understand the cosmic dimensions of good and evil, sin can no longer be seen in a frivolous way – sin is evil, evil is disgusting; it stands against God, humanity, love, creation and all that is good. It is a violation of the cosmic goals of God in his world, his dream and project. So while God loves us infinitely and wants us to live forever in a loving relationship with him, the cosmic problem of evil stands in the way.

We are all capable of good, but we are also all more than capable of evil – we are a mixture of good and evil and our motives are never fully pure. We are all sinners before a pure and holy God. We are all guilty of failing to keep the standards of God.

We have all at some time or other failed to worship God as we should.

We have all disobeyed him. We have all blasphemed his name. We have all disobeyed our parents. We have all lied, twisting and distorting the truth for personal gain. We have all stolen something in our life whether actively or passively. Actively, all of us have at some point in our lives taken something that did not belong to us. Passively, we have also participated in evil by failing to share what we have, denying others their inheritance as God's children, they being poor and we being rich. According to Jesus we have all committed adultery. Jesus said to look with lust at another person is adultery.[34] All of us have dehumanised and objectified someone else in this way at some time or another. We have all been guilty of putting others down, of saying something judgemental, of failing to give God the glory he deserves, of failing to honour others as we should. We have all judged others on some basis, whether it is by their looks, race, power, weakness or whatever. We are all, to some degree or another, participants in evil.

At this point you may feel that I am being a bit harsh. One thing you might think is that many of the horrible things humans do is due to the people involved being *sinned against*. We see this for example when a desperate person, who is a victim of injustice, commits a robbery to feed his or her family. Often violent crime is understandable to a degree if the offender is a victim of crime. This is profoundly true. Not only are we participants in wrongdoing, we are also victims of wrongdoing. In fact, the more we are sinned against, the more we are broken and marred and fall into sin.[35] Those that sinned against us are culpable before God. Yet, we too remain responsible for our sinful responses. That this is true actually reinforces the essential point: the world is broken, we are all sinners and not only are we committing sin, we are often sinned against. All this amplifies the problem of evil.

If you are not sure whether you are in fact guilty of sin in this sense you might like to turn now to appendix one (at the back of this book) which asks us to check whether we are in fact guilty of sin against the Old Testament standard of the Ten Commandments or the New Testament standard of the two Great Commandments.

We could continue this discussion looking at a host of ideals that Jesus and other Bible writers have passed on to us and we will see that again and again we are all guilty before God.[36] We are all, as the Bible puts it, sinners. We are all participants in and victims of evil, and we are all in need of being saved from this predicament.

We are a product of our sinful world, so much so that, in a sense, we can't help but sin. Even one of the founding fathers of Christianity, the Apostle Paul, laments his inability to do the good he knows he ought to do.[37] This is the universal human experience. We are sinners before a righteous, holy God. We are subject to the power of sin, enslaved under sin's power,[38] the power of evil. There seems to be no way out! 'For all have sinned, and fall short of the glory of God!'[39]

Separation

This being the case, unless the relationship is restored, we are all separated from God. You might be asking at this point why sin separates someone from God. The key concept here is the purity of God. Because he is perfect in purity, he will only dwell with us in purity. As such, he will not dwell with us *unless* we are sinless or *until* the sin within us is dealt with. There are only two ways out. One is for humans to rise above sin and evil and live pure and flawless lives, maintaining a perfect evil-free relationship with God. However, due to the power of sin that has infected the very fabric of the world, along with humanity's universal choice and penchant for doing wrong, this is not something that has been or can be achieved by anyone except Jesus (more on that later).[40] The other way out is for God to rescue us.

That being the case, apart from God reaching out to us, we are all destined to die and spend an eternity separated from him. Unless a way is found to deal with the evil that has infected us, there is no hope. We are all separated from a perfect relationship with God.

While we live on earth, this separation means that God does not dwell with us as he originally intended. We will live, but we will not be truly alive. We will face this world captive to corrupt motives and our lives will not be directed by God. We will be subject to the powers of darkness, sin in the world – all infected. There is no way out. We are all, as Paul puts it, 'prisoners of sin'.[41] We are all destined for eternal death. Paul says elsewhere, 'for the wages of sin is death, but the gift of God is eternal life through Jesus Christ our Lord.'[42] Our state of separation is ultimately eternal if it is not remedied. The New Testament makes clear from the mouths of Jesus, Paul, Peter, Jude and John that all evil will ultimately be dealt with when Jesus returns (more about that later).[43] The problem is that in the meantime we are destined for destruction, because evil is fused into the core of our being.

Is It Hopeless?

All this can seem terribly depressing. It seems on the surface that God's intention has failed. He wants an eternal relationship with each of us and he wants the world to be a glorious place of human creativity and harmony, yet not one of us can live with God forever because of his purity and our sin. Were he to let us live eternally in our flawed state, we would continue to corrupt the world we live in. If we, as impure people, were allowed into eternity then heavenly existence would be worse than earth. Imagine our human corruption combined with eternal life and eternal resources. Eternity would quickly become a scene of unimaginable eternal conflict and devastation!

In a sense then, it is hopeless. We are not capable of saving ourselves. Evil has taken hold of humanity, the world and relationships and there is no way out. The outlook is bleak *unless* God moves to save us.

In the Meantime

Perhaps you are a bit offended by this description of the state of the world and humanity. Perhaps you consider yourself a good person. In many ways I'm sure you are. Certainly, when we compare ourselves with a despotic megalomaniac like Adolf Hitler we can all appear very good. However, when we line ourselves up beside the standards of God and are truly honest about ourselves, we find that we are all flawed. Christians are no different here. If you have heard Christians claim moral superiority for themselves, I believe they are misguided. They too, like you and me, struggle with their brokenness and wrongdoing. We are not totally evil but we are marred. We are still capable of making good choices, but not with complete consistency. We are people of mixed motives, mixed intentions, and a mixture of good and bad. Hence, even though on the surface many of us are 'good people', in fact we all need salvation. Remember, God is totally pure and no evil can stand in his presence. Thus, we all stand outside this ideal relationship with him.

That being the case, I am sorry to say that it is inevitable that the world will continue to be a place in which we see terrible atrocities, natural disasters, war, poverty, oppression, sexism, racism, greed, immorality, hatred and other evils that have blighted human history since the Fall. When you look at the world and wonder why it is so fallen, it is because of the rupture that has corrupted us so that our best efforts still leave us in a perilous state. The Bible predicts an escalation in human evil as history moves towards its climax.[44] The last century had more wars and death than any before it. There were world wars, nuclear threats, natural disasters and now the threat of extremists who violate the stability of society.

Self-Realisation

I remember before my conversion to Christianity, when I was searching for God and bemoaning the state of the world – its greed, oppression, pride and spiritual futility – the truth progressively dawned on me that *I was part of the problem*. I became aware that if the world was to change, it had to start with me, with my attitudes, my actions and words. I realised I was corrupted and needed to be transformed. I recognised that there was only one person in the world I had the power to change, and that was me. This was the beginning of my path to restoration.

This is not to say that we are worthless and unloved. On the contrary, the principles of the first chapter still stand – God loves us absolutely and unconditionally, despite our flawed lives.[45] We are made in his image – despite the image being broken and flawed – and he cares for us so deeply that it hurts. He doesn't enjoy our sinfulness, our bad attitudes, deeds and words, but his love for us is relentless and he is prepared to go to extraordinary lengths to spend eternity with us.

Why Did God Allow Such a Tragedy?

Another question you might have is, 'Why would God create such a world if it would fall?' The answer is found in the principles outlined in chapter one. The first thing to say is that God created so that he would have a love-based volitional relationship with every person, and although we have fallen, that is not the end of the story. He is not a God who gives up easily. He will pursue the relationship and find a way out (see the next chapter). The second thing to realise is that God, who is all-knowing and has all knowledge across time (omniscient), knew that this fall would occur but still went ahead with his creation.[46] He did so because true awareness of freedom requires choice. In a sense, God allowed the possibility of the Fall so that freedom would be real and revealed.

We can go further. God in his omniscience actually knew that some would fall but still went ahead. Why? He did so because of his love and yearning for relationship. God, because of this love and desire to create and give freedom, considered it worthwhile to create for those who would ultimately accept his offer of relationship. God considered it better to create and risk losing some than not to create at all. We can understand this from human relationships – to risk loving is to risk rejection. The alternative is to resist relationships and die lonely. As the saying goes, 'It is better to have loved and lost than not to have loved at all.' This is the risk that every parent takes when having a child. One never knows whether the child will choose obedience, love and goodness. Yet humanity continues to have children because it is worth the risk. In the same way, God chose to create us.

Conclusion

The tragedy of human history is that while God longs to have an eternal relationship of love with every human, he will not do this because of his character of purity and our hearts of sin. The answer to the question 'What is wrong with the world?' is sin – or, even more accurately, evil. So is there a way out? Is there a way in which the original relationship can be restored? Is there a way to save people and leave them with volition, with their ability to say yes or no to God? Thankfully there is, and to this we now turn.

Questions for Reflection

1. Does the Christian explanation for evil ('the Fall') make sense to you?
2. What alternative explanation could there be that explains evil's existence?
3. Is it right to suggest humans are participants in 'evil'?

4. If humankind participates in evil, yet was originally created good, in what sense are humans good and evil? Are they 'totally depraved' as some theologians have suggested? Or are they basically good?
5. Is it fair that all humans, whatever their level of corruption, are separated from God? Do the ideas in this chapter work to explain it?
6. How do we reconcile the idea of God being omniscient ('all-knowledgeable') and sovereign, and yet still find meaning in human history? Can it be reconciled or do we live with this mystery?
7. On a personal note, what are the real issues you are dealing with? What are your weaknesses and sins?

THREE
RESTORATION

The third R in the Christian message is God's answer to this rupture or separation, his means of restoring his original intention. It answers the question, 'What is the solution?' I call the answer 'Restoration'. God has moved decisively in human history to provide a means by which the original intention of God can be restored.[1] The solution is found in Jesus Christ of Nazareth. We can say then that restoration came through Jesus Christ. This chapter will seek to explain how God has provided the means of restoration and salvation.

God's Grief

How does God feel about all of humanity being separated from him for all eternity? We get a glimpse of this in the book of Genesis, in the time leading up to the great flood of Noah.[2] The writer of Genesis says, 'The LORD saw that the wickedness of humankind was great in the earth, and that every inclination of the thoughts of their hearts was only evil continually [this is sin, evil]. And the LORD was sorry that he had made humankind on the earth, and it grieved him to his heart.'[3] Here we see the grief of God at the sin of humanity and the problem of evil. Similarly, Jesus wept over the 'fallenness' of Jerusalem.[4] We know also from the New Testament that God's Spirit can be grieved by sin, pointing to this same principle.[5] It is clear then that God grieves that humanity is separated from him. His heart is broken. He wants to spend eternity with each one of us but will not without the resolution of the problem of corruption. This fact hurts him deeply.

What's God Up To…?

God's Love

God's grief is drawn from his third and supreme attribute that we referred to in chapter one – his love. Probably the most famous verse in the Bible begins, 'For God so *loved* the world'.[6] Paul, before describing God's plan for saving us, begins by saying, 'God demonstrates his *love* for us'.[7] This is because 'God is love'[8] and 'his love endures forever'.[9] His whole being is saturated and consumed by love – that is, an attitude of mercy, grace and compassion deep in his inner core that moves him to act for the benefit of others. His love is individual – loving each one of us with a burning passion, wanting the best for us, wanting us to prosper, wanting us to express the fullness of our human potential and individuality. His love is also for the whole world – loving human society in all its positive expressions, the natural world, and loving the universe he created.

I got a glimpse of this when I became a parent. I was overwhelmingly filled with utter joy at the birth of each of our three daughters. I was filled with love for them and to this day I love nothing more than spending time with them, watching them do their thing, whether it be sport or some other activity, and living life to the full. I desperately want the best for them and dote over them, yearning for them to know only the best things in life. This human experience of love gives us a glimpse into the heart of God, whose love for us as a parent to a child is cosmically eternal in scope and passion.

God's Mission

As noted earlier in chapter one, 'love' is really a verb. It is drawn from the very heart and character of God, and is about action on behalf of others. Consequently, the love of God for every human and for his world moves him into action to save. He has seen humanity in its lost state, a fragmented society, a fallen world, and is determined to repair or 'redeem' the situation. So it is that God the creator has become God the saviour.[10]

The process of salvation began immediately after the Fall. This love is first seen in God's response to the sin of Adam and Eve. Note how, despite their sin, he clothed them – an act of extraordinary grace to the disobedient pair.[11] He did not kill them, but expelled them from the garden, still allowing them to become the parents of humanity. When all people crumbled into almost complete sin and decadence and he brought the flood so that humanity could start over again, he ensured the continuation of human life by saving Noah and his family.[12] When, at the Tower of Babel, humanity began to work together to create such levels of evil that they threatened to destroy themselves and God's intention, God scattered them and confused their language in order to limit evil.[13] Then he chose Abraham and Sarah to be the parents of the nation of Israel, through whom God would prepare the way for the restoration of his original intention (more on that later).[14]

Through the history of Abraham's family, Israel, God continued to protect his people. He saved them from famine in Egypt[15] and delivered them miraculously from the merciless oppression of Rameses II.[16] He led them through the wilderness[17] and gave them a law on which to order their lives.[18] Then he gave them a land 'flowing with milk and honey', allowing them to conquer the utterly sinful inhabitants of Canaan.[19] He interacted with his people for over 1400 years, ensuring that they did not self-destruct, and watched over them as a nation.[20]

He did this with one fundamental purpose in mind – to prepare the way for the moment when he would act decisively in human history to save humanity. The Old Testament history of Israel culminates in the coming of the 'Messiah' – Jesus Christ. The Messiah is the 'anointed one' or 'the Christ' who Jews believed would be a royal descendant of the Hebrew king David (1040-970 BC) and who would restore God's work on the earth.[21] Everything in the Old Testament points to this event. The sacrifice system with its complex requirements (established early in Israel's history) prepared the way for the manner of Jesus' death, by crucifixion. Set against the backdrop of this system, Jesus became the ultimate sacrifice for the world.[22] Individual moments in the story of Israel – such as when Abraham was apparently told by God to sacrifice his son Isaac until God supplied a ram in his place – foreshadowed and prepared the way for Jesus.[23]

The temple that had been built in Jerusalem points to Jesus as a 'living temple'. Not only does Jesus fulfil this, but individual Christians are now described as 'the temple of the Holy Spirit', as are the people of God as a united body.[24] Jesus ultimately fulfilled the system of priesthood that operated in the Old Testament, and became the 'eternal high priest'.[25] He is also the new and final Passover lamb who takes away the sins of the world.[26] The law given to Moses on Mt Sinai prepared the way for the Messiah because through the law, people became aware of their sin and their failure to keep the law.[27] This law made people aware of their need for salvation.

There are a number of specific prophecies predicting the coming of the Messiah, fulfilled with remarkable accuracy in the coming of Jesus. These include his birth,[28] where he would live and minister,[29] his ministry and miracles,[30] his suffering and death[31] and his resurrection.[32] The scattering of the people of Israel through being conquered by a number of other civilisations (known as the 'Diaspora'), and the fact that Israel was under the power of Rome at the time of Christ, enabled the message about Jesus to spread quickly through scattered Jewish communities and throughout the Roman Empire. It was as if all of history and creation itself was readied, holding its breath for the coming of the one who would save the world.

The First Coming of Jesus Christ

The moment of God's salvation came when Jesus was sent from God. He was the long-awaited Jewish Messiah, but he also came to save the entire world.

Many people focus on his death and resurrection as the key issue in terms of the restoration of the relationship between God and humanity. This is correct in terms of the dynamics of salvation, but in fact his whole life is of great significance.

His Birth

Jesus' birth is described as a miracle. First, Matthew and Luke tell us that he was the child of a virgin, mothered by a Jewish woman named Mary and fathered by God through his Spirit.[33] Secondly, his birth results in the miracle of incarnation, meaning to become flesh (*in-carno* = 'in flesh') – that is, he became human and part of God's creation.[34] Jesus was 'God become flesh'. The idea that God became 'matter' and participated in this world is an amazing enough concept. That he became a baby, the most vulnerable of all living beings, in a woman's womb, the most dangerous place in the ancient world, is totally astonishing. Particularly when one considers that the first believers, like contemporary devoted Muslims, had been radical monotheists who did not anticipate such an event; that many of them believed in Jesus at all is almost unbelievable. The fact that Jesus came to earth as a baby illustrates that God chooses to save us not by an external intervention of cosmic military power, but from the inside by love and gentleness.

His Ministry

Jesus' life and message teaches us a lot about the nature of God. He is evidence of the heart of God and God's desire that humanity would be restored. We can identify at least six key dimensions to Jesus' ministry: gathering people to community, being a friend to marginalised people, providing compassionate care for people in need, healing the sick and the demonised, performing miracles, and preaching with the aim of pointing people towards salvation (i.e. calling people to put their faith in him).

His work was the beginning of a new community of humanity as God intended. His miracles all point in different ways to the ultimate restoration that will result from his life, death and resurrection. When he miraculously provided food for the hungry, this pointed to the end of poverty, inequality and famine. The healings he performed pointed to the end of sickness and human suffering. When he cast out demons, that pointed to the final defeat of evil. When he performed nature miracles, like calming a storm or walking on water, these pointed to his power over the created order, and his ability to put an end to chaos and finally restore God's creation. His life and work set the example of what true humanity is like – a life of love devoted to the physical, emotional, social and spiritual needs of others. He came to restore, to establish the world as God always intended it to be.

His Teaching

Jesus taught us how to live. His message can be boiled down to two essential concepts: to love God with all that we are, and to love one another the way we all long to be loved.[35] This is the essence of authentic humanity – the love of God and the love of others. Jesus came to restore the original relationship of love that we talked about in chapter one. One of the greatest passages in the Bible is Matthew's summary of Jesus' teaching called the 'Sermon on the Mount'. This gives insight into the teaching of Jesus on spiritual life, family, care for the poor and human relationships.[36] It reflects God's dream for his restored world.

The Servant King

When Jesus turned up, the people of Israel were desperate for a Messiah. They yearned for someone like King David to come and defeat their foreign oppressors. By this time in their history, they had been conquered by a number of international powers: the Assyrians, the Babylonians, the Medo-Persians, the Greeks and now the Romans. They wanted Israel to be established in its own right as a united nation under God's reign, subject to the Law, and sovereign over the world. Their hope was that their enemies would be vanquished and that all nations would be subjugated to the power of God and Israel, bringing their wealth into Jerusalem.

Jesus turned this concept on its head. He did not come with political and military might, but instead came with the attitude of a servant.[37] He renounced violence and avoided the possibility of his followers making him into a king and declaring war on the Roman authorities.[38] When his disciples recognised him as Messiah, he accepted their confession but instantly told them that he would be rejected, suffer and die.[39] This was not expected – the Messiah was not expected to suffer and die, but rather, to end suffering and inflict death on God's enemies.

Jesus told his disciples that they too must live lives of service, renouncing violence and military might. They were to 'take up their crosses and follow' in his footsteps.[40] They had to live for the good of others. After this he continued to heal the sick, befriend the marginalised and serve humanity. When he was falsely arrested and crucified he forgave his killers.[41] He went to his death refusing to resort to the power of the sword, preferring the true power of the universe – the power of love. By his suffering and death, he revealed that God is saving his world through sacrifice, selflessness, suffering and service.[42] Jesus is a king, but he is a servant king.

His Death

The death of Jesus is the crunch point of all human history. At the cross, God in Christ experienced the full extent of human suffering. This is a phenomenal concept – God the Son, the creator of all that we know; God the Son, all powerful; God the Son, all-knowing… killed! Crucified![43] Flogged, beaten, ridiculed, crowned with thorns and nailed to a cross until he suffocated to death. As we will see later, this death was on our behalf. It was the means by which he solved the problem of evil and restored the original intended relationship of God with humanity. Later we will discuss in more detail how Jesus' death and resurrection paved the way for human salvation.

His Resurrection

Without the resurrection, Jesus' death would be a sad and essentially meaningless event[44] – just another good man killed unnecessarily and unjustly. Amazingly, a few days after his death, despite the presence of a Roman guard and a large rock blocking the entrance, his tomb was found to be empty – the body was gone. Jesus was then sighted on ten separate occasions by various women,[45] by disciples in different places at different times, by Paul and even by 500 at one time.[46]

The first witnesses were so convinced of the reality of their experience and that Jesus had risen from the dead that they refused to recant even when persecuted, tortured and put to death.[47] They were so sure that Jesus had risen that they went into a Greco-Roman world that philosophically despised the body and the notion of a bodily resurrection, and counter-culturally preached that Jesus had risen in bodily form. They suffered and died for this for the first three centuries of Christian history (and many more since).

The best explanation of the existing evidence is that Jesus did indeed rise from the dead.[48] This makes Jesus utterly unique amongst history's greatest leaders, religious and otherwise. It is this event that points to Jesus as the saviour of the world and makes sense of his terrible death.

His Ascension and Exaltation

In the book of Acts, Luke records that some time after Jesus rose from the dead, he returned to heaven, ascending into the clouds before the eyes of his disciples.[49] This shows that Jesus, although still human and yet also God, never died again. Rather, he rose to eternal life to reign as our Lord over all creation.[50] He is now the Lord of all, living in heaven, ruling with God the Father and God the Spirit. The person and power that lived within him, the Spirit of God, is now present with us on earth, empowering, restoring, saving, leading, guiding, inspiring and more.

Restoration

So why did Jesus do all this? Jesus died to restore the relationship between God and humanity. He died to solve the problem that our sin has separated us from a pure God. How does this restoration work?

As we said in chapter two ('Rupture'), unless saved, all humanity stands before God in a state of separation. Unless there is some external intervention, because of our universal participation in evil, we are all separated from God and his world is corrupted.

God in his purity and with his justice will not allow this situation to continue. Because of his purity, he will deal with evil to restore the perfection of his creation. Because of his justice, he will remove evil because it is an affront to him and must be dealt with. Again, because of his justice, it is necessary to punish evil.

Some people struggle with this notion of punishment. However, take a step back and consider why evil deserves to be punished. At its heart, evil is the drive to rebel against God and destroy the beauty and goodness of his creation. When we participate in evil we align ourselves with the destructive forces behind the intent of evil. God will not, and should not, allow this to continue. Such rebellion and destruction deserves to be punished.

If a man went amok today, running rampant through the nation, blowing up houses, killing innocent people and destroying everything we hold dear in this nation, should the government stand by and allow this to go on? Of course not. Rather than turn a blind eye, it would stop this person and punish him – and deservedly so. His punishment should be extreme because he has destroyed beauty and goodness, and has robbed us of life, peace, safety and security. In the same way, God will punish evil. This includes not only the extremes of human evil (such as Hitler and others who perpetrated the Holocaust) but all humanity who, without exception (aside from Jesus himself), have participated in evil. Everything that is evil or partially evil stands condemned before God.

This means we (that's me and you), right now, unless saved in some way, are condemned before God and destined to suffer the same fate as all evil – destruction and punishment. The propensity for evil is forged into who we are. This includes the most heinous of sinners from Hitler to Pol Pot, through to the most righteous person who has ever lived (aside from Jesus) – even 'good' people have at times failed to honour God completely and have participated to some extent in evil.

At the heart of Christianity is the truth that Jesus solved the problem of evil by dying on the cross. In essence he took all evil upon himself, all the sin of the world, all the punishment, all the judgment, all its destruction, and paid the price for it. His mode of death – the humiliation and pain of Roman crucifixion – is appropriate. It is as if Jesus took the worst the world could throw at him. But he never sinned himself.[51] He never participated in evil and yet, he was unjustly tried, cruelly beaten and violently crucified. By doing this, he took the penalty of death upon himself, despite never sinning himself.

As we saw earlier, sin leads to death.[52] Therefore, this suggests that where there is no sin, there is no death. In Jesus' case, that is exactly the effect of what occurred. He lived a sinless life, died a sinless man, and so he rose from the dead. Because of this unjust death, death was defeated, sin was dealt with and a way of being saved was opened up. His death means that we can now be restored to a relationship with God, despite our sin.

Ways of Understanding this Process

This is a difficult concept to explain because, in some ways, it is unexplainable. No one is capable of fully understanding how a cosmic being who has all power, all love and all knowledge, and is able to exist simultaneously across all time and space while at the same time existing outside of time and space, could become human, live, die and rise from the dead. Then, somehow, his death becomes a means of gaining salvation for humanity! It is certainly remarkable to consider that a sinless man can die and save a sinful world. Thankfully, the Bible writers use a number of different ways to explain the concept. Their explanations help us to understand how it works, even if we can never fully comprehend or explain it.

Atoned = 'Made One'. One of the words used to describe what Jesus did is the 'atonement' (meaning 'making one'). It has become a general term used by Christians to describe what Jesus did on the cross. The need to become 'one' of course relates to reversing the separation of

God and humanity caused by sin. In the Old Testament, atonement was achieved through animal sacrifices.[53] In the New Testament, atonement is achieved through the death of Jesus who died to restore the relationship between God and humanity, to make God and humanity one.

Justified = 'Declared Righteous', Pardoned or Acquitted. Another way of describing the problem of our separation due to evil, is through the idea of a law court. It is as if we are in court standing before God (the judge of the world) and are found guilty of committing evil. We must pay the price that has been set down as the punishment for evil: eternal separation from God, the irrevocable and total removal of evil from his presence and created order.

However, through Jesus, God provided for our guilt by Jesus taking the punishment on our behalf. We call this 'penal-substitution'.[54] In this way of looking at why Jesus died on the cross, God is the judge who pronounces us guilty, then steps down from the dock and pays our fine. He goes to jail or takes the death penalty for us. Then, after doing the time for our crime, he returns to the dock and pronounces us free on the basis of what he has done. We are guilty, but we are acquitted or pardoned because our punishment is fulfilled.

We are thus 'declared righteous' (justified, guilt-free) even though we remain in one sense unrighteous and will continue to do unrighteous things because of our fallen humanness – justified not because of what *we* have done, but because of what *Jesus* has done.[55] He fulfilled all God's laws and we are declared righteous before God because of him. This pardon or acquittal is undeserved. Christians call this 'grace' – the wonderful notion of the undeserved love and mercy of God demonstrated in the death of Jesus for our sin and evil.

Reconciled = 'Declared to be Friends of God'. The socio-political language of reconciliation is also used in the New Testament to explain the problem of our separation. In this way of describing the cross, before Jesus came we were all enemies of God – a bit like an enemy nation in a time of war. This is not necessarily because we are particularly aggressive toward God in an intentional way, but because all evil is the enemy of God and we are participants in that evil. However, when Jesus died, he reconciled us to God and removed our enmity. That being the case, we are no longer enemies of God, but his friends[56] – the intended relationship is restored.[57] Rather than experiencing the wrath that all evil deserves, because of what Jesus has done, we are considered friends of God forever. Not because of our perfection or goodness, but because of Jesus' death and resurrection. This is the restoration of the original intention of God.

The notion of reconciliation is not confined to the reconciliation of God and people, but of all people and things. The desire of God is that this reconciliation will flow to all people, restoring the society of humankind and bringing peace. This means the end of all conflict and broken relationships. Christians are reconciled to God and are then called to work towards the reconciliation of all relationships. Reconciliation also relates to all of creation. When Christ died, he died for the world, to reconcile all things to God. This is God's big plan to restore his entire broken world, including all of humanity and the natural order. It is God's intention that Christians will work towards this aim.[58]

Sanctified = 'Declared to be Holy and Pure'. The effect of the cross is also described in the New Testament through the religious concept of holiness. Before Jesus came, we were unholy, impure sinners compared with God's glorious purity. Jesus, through the cross, exchanged our sin and unholiness for his purity. Even though we are not holy or perfectly pure, we are declared holy through what Jesus did.[59] Thus being 'sanctified' (made holy) is an event that occurs at salvation. We are washed clean 'through the blood of Jesus' – that is, through his death on the cross. The notion of sanctification is also described as the process of 'becoming holy'. That is, after being declared holy, we are to seek to 'be holy' – to live a life that pleases God in purity and grace – to be steadily transformed into the people that God wants us to be.[60]

Adopted = 'Accepted as God's Children'. As discussed in chapter one, God's purpose in creation was to form a family relationship with humanity. He would be our ultimate parent, and we his children, living together in a relationship of love. In chapter two we saw that this relationship has been tragically ruptured. When Jesus came, as the Son of God, he set out to re-establish a new creation and family. He was always the Son of God, but his flawless life, death and resurrection enables humanity to be restored to the family of God. Through Christ we can be *adopted* into God's family as his children.[61] This means we are given all the privileges of being children of God – heirs to all that God has created for us.[62] Therefore, we are expected to be like the best possible family – loving one another as God has loved us.

We should not confuse this with the idea that we will have perfect lives. Paul warns us that, as adopted children living in an imperfect world seeking to work for goodness, we will face struggles and suffering just as all humans and Jesus himself did. However, as we live in this family, we will experience God's life sustaining us through his power. We are also promised a glorious reward for our service.[63]

Regenerated = 'Born Again'. You may have heard of the phrase 'born again Christian'. The concept of being born again is closely related to the notion of adoption. John tells us that anyone who believes in Jesus and receives him is given the right to become a child of God.[64] This isn't achieved through being born into a relationship with God because of our parents' faith or our culture, but through what the Holy Spirit does.

When a person expresses faith in Christ, the Holy Spirit enters that person's inner being (or heart), guaranteeing them eternal life.[65] This Spirit regenerates the inner life of the person and is the crux of the relationship with God. The person is 'born again' or 'born from above' – that is, born into the heavenly family of God. It is like a second birth. Paul, writing to Titus, expresses this idea saying that God saves us through the 'washing of rebirth and renewal by the Holy Spirit'.[66]

Crucified/resurrected = 'We Die and Rise in Christ'. Another way Paul describes what Jesus has done is that we participate *in Christ*, including his cross and resurrection.[67] Before Jesus came, we were dead in our sins.[68] Paul describes this as being 'in Adam' (i.e. under the effect of what Adam and Eve did).[69] Because of our participation in sin and corruption, while we may feel very much alive physically, we are spiritually separated from God and therefore 'dead'. However, through the principle of substitution and exchange (that we will examine in more detail below), we can be 'in Christ' rather than 'in Adam'. This means that, in a spiritual sense, we were in Jesus when he died on the cross. His death then becomes our death. So Paul can say, 'I have been crucified with Christ.'[70] Our old life of sin is extinguished in Jesus' death.

Similarly, as noted above, we are in Jesus' resurrection. This has two dimensions. First, at the point of committing ourselves to Jesus, we are spiritually resurrected with Christ, 'born again' as children of God.[71] However, aside from this internal transformation, we remain as we are in our mortal bodies. Secondly, being in Christ anticipates our future bodily resurrection where our present bodies are raised from the dead and become incorruptible. In the present, although we remain sinners after our salvation, the process of the exchange of our sin for Jesus' righteousness continues dealing with our sin to allow us to remain children of God and pure in his sight. We are seen by God through the 'lens' of Jesus' perfection. For Paul, living in Christ means that, while we await a future resurrection of the body, in the present we will face suffering and struggle. However, we will do so with the power of God sustaining us in our inner being.

Redeemed = 'Bought out of Slavery'. Another description of salvation is taken from the slave culture that was part of everyday life in the first century setting. Slaves were the labour force of the Roman Empire. In these terms, before Jesus came, we were slaves to sin, trapped in a world infected by evil to its core. We were unable to get free from the grip of corruption. When Jesus died and rose he paid the price of our freedom and bought us out of slavery. We were set free, as a slave could be set free, for the right price – this is done by Jesus paying the ransom for sin.[72]

Forgiven = 'Sin Pardoned'. A common way of describing salvation is through the idea of 'forgiveness'. We are all trapped in the shame and guilt of broken relationships and of failing to please God. After Jesus came, the path to freedom and peace is found in his mercy and forgiveness.[73] Because Jesus died for us, we can be totally forgiven, experiencing the joy of complete freedom and peace with God.[74] Thus, our brokenness is dealt with by Jesus on the cross.

This does not mean all the consequences of our mistakes are gone. If a person has committed murder, that person should still do the time. The hurt we have caused may remain as bad as ever. However, because of what Christ has done, no matter how terrible what we have done is, God will forgive us. This is hard to understand in the case of a perpetrator of terrible atrocities. However, this is the extent of God's grace, our sin and evil, no matter how heinous, will be forgiven if we come to God in repentance, contrition and penitence (i.e. if we are truly sorry).

Saved = 'Delivered from Sin'. The summary term that the New Testament uses for the concept of being saved is 'salvation'. Salvation means being saved *from* something and *into* something. Take for example those saved in the September 11 tragedy in the USA in 2001 – they were saved *from* death as the buildings crashed to the ground, and they were saved *into* the rest of their lives.

Through Christ's death, we have been saved *from* evil and sin and all its consequences, death and eternal destruction (i.e. separation from God). We have been saved *into* God's family, his blessing and inheritance. We are saved into God's new creation. Jesus said that the reason he came was 'to seek and *save* the lost'.[75] Paul tells us that there are three aspects to this salvation: we *have* been saved,[76] we are *being* saved,[77] and we *will be* saved.[78] This means that we are saved at the point we enter into a relationship with Jesus as Saviour and Lord (see chapter five), we are in the process of being saved as we walk with Jesus through life, and we will be saved when he returns (see chapter four).

Restored Humanity = 'A New People of God'. The concepts we have looked at so far have focussed on the aspects of salvation applicable to us as individuals. But there are several other more collective notions that are important to grasp. The first is that we are called to be a part of a group of people who are central to God's new creation. When we become Christians we are not merely saved so that we can have a pietistic personal relationship with God. As we believe in Jesus, we become part of God's people, who are supposed to reflect the principles of the dream and project of God as seen in chapter one (i.e. love, unity, community, harmony, joy, peace and more).

This group of people is called many things in the Bible and described in many images. It is the 'people of God', 'the body of Christ', 'the temple of the Spirit', 'the family of God', 'the bride of Christ' and, most often, 'the church'. The New Testament does not consider the church to be a building, but rather a group of people. Jesus came to establish this new people group and when you become a believer you are instantly a part of it. The church is far from perfect and has failed to live up to its calling on many occasions. But the ideal stands and when we join it through faith, we are called to participate in it alongside others, expressing God's love and grace to each other and to the world. God's dream is that all humanity will become his people. For this reason, we are called to live among the rest of humanity, demonstrating the glorious freedom, love and creativity of being God's children to draw them in.

The purpose of Jesus coming was not just to establish the church, but also to restore God's overall intention for human society. Every trace of the fragmentation of human society can be linked back to the fall of humanity. The intention is that, through Jesus coming to earth, human relationships will be restored.

At the Fall, Adam and Eve's relationship was instantly corrupted. They fought over who was to blame for their mistake (see chapter two). Their sons fought, and Cain killed Abel,[79] setting a pattern of sibling rivalry that has continued ever since. As we read the subsequent narrative of Genesis, we see an increase in violence, hatred, jealousy and impurity, culminating in the purification of the world through the Flood.[80] After the Flood, humankind once again returned to pre-Flood behaviours and humanity was ultimately scattered and fragmented because of their unbridled evil.[81] Ever since those early days of human society, history has been blighted by the consequences of the Fall – such as war, murder, destruction and disintegration.

Jesus' arrival on earth is the culmination of God's plan for restoration. It was initiated with Jesus who, as we have seen, lived a perfect life of love and mercy[82] reaching out to the lost,[83] hanging out with the marginalised and most sinful people in society,[84] and inviting them into the family of God.

He called for a new ethic of love for all humanity – most especially through the call to 'love your neighbour as yourself'.[85] He declared that this would be the defining mark of his people. He called for unconditional love by which we love not for what we receive in return, but for love's sake. He went as far as saying, 'love your enemies' – a totally radical and scandalous notion in a world of enmity.[86] Jesus called for people to emulate his love. The ultimate demonstration of this love was his death in which, because of his unbridled affection for humanity, he willingly gave himself for us by dying on a cross.[87] Paul writes, 'God demonstrates his love for us in this: while we were yet sinners, Christ died for us.'[88] John writes, 'Greater love has no one than this, that he lay down his life for his friends.'[89] He also writes, 'for God so loved the world, that he gave his one and only Son, that whoever believes in him, shall not perish but have everlasting life.'[90]

When we believe in Christ, his Spirit fills us,[91] and we receive a new power to love. As the Spirit empowers and transforms us from within, the evidence of the 'fruit of the Spirit' is increasingly evident in our lives – such things as love, peace and joy.[92] It is God's dream that his people will live in perfect harmony, loving one another. The church is designed to be a microcosm of heaven on earth, a community of God's people, full of love for one another, without need, demonstrating to the world what God always intended. It is to be a gathering of people from all classes of society, men and women, of all ethnicities. In this community, there should be unity and no rank or status.[93] Sadly, it has rarely fulfilled its potential throughout history. Nevertheless, God's plan for his church still remains. It is God's hope that this love will spread, this community of love will grow, drowning evil, lightening up the darkness and transforming the world. This is the dream and project of God.

Restored World = 'A New Heavens and a New Earth' or 'A New Creation'.
While God wants to save all individuals – including you and me – and

establish the church on earth, there is even more that he plans to do. The coming of Jesus was not *just* to save those who are separated from God so that they could be formed into a new group of people. His ultimate dream and project is much bigger – he wants to restore the whole world. It is this project that we are swept up into when we say yes to God.

At a micro level, this plan starts with us being 'converted' individually as we accept God. His Spirit enters us and then we are to go about our lives assisted by him, seeking to bring God's love into the world by our attitudes, actions and carefully spoken words. We join other Christians and live together in unity and love. However, we are also told to remain in the world, working as we worked before, using all our God-given gifts, our various personalities, creativity, intelligence, talents, time and money to make the world the place God intended it to be. We do this as we share Christ's love and message so that others can also be saved. God will ultimately fully transform this broken world – it is our job to begin this work by bringing the hope of heaven to earth.

This is what some call the *Missio Dei* (Latin, meaning 'mission of God') and what I like to call God's '*cosmission*'. This word comes from two words, the Greek *kosmos* indicating 'the world, all creation' and the Latin *missio* meaning 'send'. That is, God's mission on earth is to restore his world to his original intention. More than that, God wants to restore human relationships and community – whether they be families, communities, cities or nations – to his hope of a world full of love. He wants creation itself to be cared for, the fragile balance of the natural world sustained as humanity uses the resources he has provided creatively and productively. He wants every part of his world restored to his original intention. God cares deeply about this world and his cosmission is to restore it!

Jesus' favourite way of speaking about his own ministry was in terms

Restoration

of the 'Kingdom of God' or the 'Kingdom of Heaven'.[94] He declared, 'the Kingdom of God is near'[95] and 'the Kingdom of God is among you.'[96] By these statements Jesus was declaring that he was the king of a new kind of kingdom that was being established on planet earth.

Paul spoke of Jesus as 'Lord' – God come to his people – the true Caesar over the world – head of the heavenly community on earth. When we believe in Christ, we enter this kingdom. As we have seen, this is not just about personal salvation but the transformation of the whole of life. From our locus as God's people, we are to go out into every nook and cranny of the world as led by God and be agents of positive transformation.

This means not only that Jesus came as Saviour, but he also came to the earth as God the Son in human form to restore his world.[97] Hence, the Kingdom was inaugurated – God's reign was established on earth.[98] This one man, God the Son, was sent from God to begin the restoration of planet earth back to his original intention at creation. Jesus himself described the Kingdom of God as being like a mustard seed, the smallest garden seed known to the first century Palestinian audience, which grows into a large tree.[99] He also described the Kingdom as a force that works through the world like yeast works through dough, causing it to rise.[100] Jesus said that Christians are like salt, which gives food flavour and preserves it.[101] Similarly, Jesus is described as the 'light of the world',[102] and Christians are called to carry this light,[103] taking it into the darkness of a fallen world.

The Kingdom thus began with Jesus and continues to grow quietly through people like you and me. Jesus predicted in his story of the mustard seed that the Kingdom will become the biggest of all garden plants (i.e. the dominant ideology / religion of the world – 'the biggest of all trees'). He said the nations would come and 'perch' in its branches like 'the birds of the air'. This has indeed happened in human history – from a group of twelve disciples, the Kingdom of God became the dominant faith / ideology on planet earth, and continues to be to this day.[104]

When Jesus gathered a group of disciples around him, he did not choose politicians, military or religious leaders, but instead took humble 'average' men and women – fishermen, tax-collectors, soldiers,[105] and women from a range of backgrounds (including some men and women from highly dubious pasts).[106] Over the course of three years, Jesus taught these disciples about the Kingdom and how to be subjects of the King. Then they were sent out to declare that God's kingdom had come so that the world would recognise that Jesus was the King and their way to salvation.

The disciples were warned that their task would not be easy. They were told to go with an attitude of service. They were not to take up arms or find power at the point of a sword or by military force. Rather, they were to work through the pattern set down by Jesus dying on the cross – loving all people, serving, sacrificing themselves, suffering and even dying to see God's plan come to pass. This they did and, through this, Christianity changed the world.

The full intention of Jesus is bigger than saving people from darkness, sin, death and judgement. It involves the restoration of the whole world. It is a huge rebuilding project – the world lies in ruins and his people will restore it. It reminds me of those who, after the end of World War 2, began work all over Europe rebuilding towns and cities devastated by conflict.

The full project involves God's people moving out into every part of society, whether it be the world of politics, education, health, the arts, sciences, sport and leisure, or social networks and families, to see the world be as God intended.

The New Testament tells us that because of God's determination to allow human volition (as we saw earlier) and his refusal to exert his rule with power, this project will not be fully achieved before the return of Christ. However, this should in no way hinder our determination to work as 'cosmic transformers' with God. Amazing things can be achieved through selfless service, suffering and sacrifice – as seen in the example of Jesus.

What begins at a micro level with salvation in the life of the individual, is ultimately expressed at a macro level through God's plan for the whole of creation. At the heart of God's mission is of course the goal that all people will believe in Jesus. For it is only when a person comes to faith in him that they experience the restoration of their relationship with God, that they gain the power to live for good and not self, that their full potential is realised and their reason for living achieved. God's people then have a job to do: to change the world through living out their God-given destiny and potential through the power and leading of God. This will involve us going out into every corner of the world to bring about God's purposes. It will involve us using every bit of our God-given creativity with love, to see the world become the wonderful place God has in mind.

The Heart of the Matter...

As mentioned at the beginning of this chapter, in reality God's salvation is unable to be fully and adequately explained. Ultimately, it is too vast to get our human brains around. After all, how is a person saved by the Son of God becoming human and dying for them? Yet this is how God chose to save the world. It's an ingenious salvation. Think about the other options God had.

First, he could have chosen to save us by forcing us to believe, or by *over-*

powering our will and removing our ability to not believe. If he had done this we would have become robots or automatons and would have no capacity to love him volitionally. This would violate the principle of freedom that is inherent in genuine love (see chapter one).

Secondly, God could have chosen to save us by *overlooking* all evil, including our sin and allow all humanity and creation to live forever in a corrupted and flawed state. However, if he had done this, evil would remain etched into us and this world eternally, and it would stand in opposition to good forever, never to be removed. Satan himself would be an eternal being. As such the whole universe would potentially implode upon itself – evil and chaos would triumph.

Thirdly, he could have chosen to save us by *overthrowing* evil in an instant – a complete extermination without attempting to resolve the problem of human corruption. But if he were going to do this, he would have done so the moment Adam and Eve first sinned. All humanity and the world would have ceased to exist. As such God's intention of a loving relationship with free volitional intelligent beings would fail (i.e. no one would be saved).

Rather than these alternatives, God chose a way that achieved our salvation while preserving our volition. He did it by *overcoming* our evil through his own sacrifice, suffering, love and mercy. It is a simple concept on one level, yet incredibly complex on another. God's method is achieved through an exchange that I call the *cosmic exchange of the cross*.[107] It works like this:

- Jesus takes *upon himself* our sin, evil, death and judgement, and himself pays the consequences we should have suffered.
- Jesus then gives *to us* his life, righteousness and purity, and we live forever as friends of God.

He is prepared to suffer our judgement, our destruction and our punishment so that we can be free – not because of what we have done, but because of what he has done!

So it is that you and I can be saved through Jesus Christ. God in Jesus has given all humanity the means by which they can be saved. This of course raises the question of what we have to do to acquire this salvation. However, before we turn to the answer, there is one more aspect of what God is up to on planet earth we need to look at first. In the next chapter we will talk about God's future plans for this world, for his people and how evil will finally be destroyed.

Conclusion

So, what is the solution? The answer is Jesus Christ. Not just Jesus meek and mild who looks down from stained glass windows and out of children's picture books, but Jesus who was God, who was born into human history, who became a man, who ministered God's love and message, who was rejected by his people, who loved his enemies, yet was crucified and who rose again to his true cosmic glory.

Amazingly, God chose to save the world not through an immense irresistible power that overthrows evil at a single stroke (as so many expected and, indeed, still do today), but through the suffering, death and resurrection of his own son. When we return to our initial question then, 'What's God up to on planet earth?' we find that God is up to saving his world through Jesus. He is seeking to restore the world to its original purpose.

He is longing to see every human he so lovingly created restored to an eternal life-giving relationship with him. He wants to see human society restored to harmony and love. He is working to see his whole created world restored to his initial intent of glorious creativity, wonder and awe.

This brings us inevitably to the next question, 'When will this finally come to its conclusion?'

Questions for Reflection

1. How does it make you feel when you think that God is deeply grieved by injustice, evil and sin?
2. What do you think about Jesus? Who do you think he was or is?
3. What do you think of the idea of the King of the world, the Messiah, the Son of God, coming to earth and dying on a cross? Why did God do it this way? How else may God have done it and still have been true to his character?
4. Consider the transformation that took place in the lives of the first Jewish disciples after their experience of his resurrection? Can it be explained in other ways that make sense?
5. What is your favourite way of explaining the process of the death of Christ that we looked at (e.g. justified, reconciled, etc)?
6. Consider the church in the world. What should it look like? How has it failed? What must it do?
7. In light of this restoration, how should Christians relate to the world?

RETURN

So far we have looked at three R's of the gospel. The first is *'relationship'*: 'God made me to have a relationship with him' (we are created to have an eternal relationship of love with the God of the universe). Secondly, *'rupture'*: 'but the rupture came through human sin' (the wonderful ideal of a relationship with God, with each other and our world has been ruptured. Therefore, all humanity, because of their participation in evil through human sin, is separated from God because of his awesome purity). Thirdly, *'restoration'*: 'restoration came through Jesus Christ' (God moved decisively out of his love to send his son to be born a human, to demonstrate his character and grace, to die on the cross in our place, and to rise from the dead). In his death and resurrection, Jesus overcame the power of death and evil, and now offers to exchange our sin and evil for his righteousness so that, despite the fact that we are still sinners, we can stand before God, pure and righteous in a loving and open relationship with him. His desire is to see all human relationships and the entire creation restored.

In this chapter, we will jump ahead through time to the end of the gospel story – here we encounter the *'return'*, the fourth 'R' of the Christian message. The 'Return' refers to the climax of human history when Jesus comes back to earth.

We saw in chapters one and two that an understanding of the beginning of humanity is required to make sense of the Christian message. In the same way, full comprehension of the overall message requires an understanding of the culmination of human history. The New Testament has at its heart the conviction that the world as we know it will come to a glorious climax at the return of Christ. This chapter answers the question, 'When and how will it all end?'

The End of the Age

The worldview of the Bible is based on a 'two age' scheme – the 'age of this world' and the 'age of the world to come'.[1] In other words, history is divided between human life on earth in the present space-time experience and a future dimension that will begin with the return of Christ.[2] The present age in which we find ourselves is the age of human existence and history. It began at creation and will culminate at the return of Jesus. Since the Fall, and the rupture of the relationship with God, this period has been in many ways a time of darkness, dominated by the power of evil and sin. Human history has also been plagued by war, death, oppression, poverty, suffering, pain and torment. It is an age in which Satan, the 'god of this age', wreaks havoc.[3]

It is not all bad however, for God has been at work in human history as well. Just as there are and have been times of terrible chaos, there have also been great people, and great instances of love, victory and justice. While the world is dark, the light continues to shine in the darkness.

Into this age, God sent his Son Jesus to die on the cross to restore the relationship between God, humanity and the world. Jesus' first arrival was, in a sense, the beginning of the end – the arrival of God's salvation, the end intervening into the centre of history. The Bible is emphatic – there will be an end to this age, and around this end a series of events will occur.

The Return of Christ

The key event that marks the end of the age is the return of Christ. The return is clearly foreshadowed in Luke's account of Jesus' 'ascension', when he was taken into heaven after he rose from the dead. In the Gospel of Luke we read:

> After he (Jesus) said this, he was *taken up before their very eyes, and a cloud hid him from their sight.* They were looking intently up into the sky as he was going, when suddenly two men dressed in white stood beside them. 'Men of Galilee,' they said, 'why do you stand here looking into the sky? This same Jesus, who has been taken from you into heaven, will *come back in the same way* you have seen him go into heaven.'[4]

This return in the clouds of heaven is also referred to at other points in the New Testament. Jesus himself declared, 'at that time men and women will see the Son of Man (that is Jesus) *coming in clouds* with great power and glory.'[5] Paul too, when speaking of the return says, 'for the Lord himself will *come down from heaven*, with a loud command, with the voice of the archangel and with the trumpet call of God.'[6]

These verses teach that Jesus the man still exists in heaven. He still has his human body, now raised in an incorruptible eternal form, God the Son. His ongoing existence is called his 'exaltation' or 'session' in which he is seated 'at the right hand of God'.[7] An example of this is found in a sermon by Peter recorded in Acts where he says that Jesus has been 'exalted to the right hand of God, he has received from the Father the promised Holy Spirit and has poured out what you now see and hear.'[8] This is a figurative way of saying that Jesus is now raised up to the highest place beside God the Father, supreme ruler of the universe.

Paul puts it this way: 'therefore God exalted him to the highest place and gave him the name that is above every name.'[9] The name that is above every name is 'Lord'. This is a radical statement! It implies that Jesus is Lord of the world. First century Romans and Greeks saw Caesar as the lord of the Empire. But Paul is daringly declaring from a prison cell *in Rome* at the mercy of Caesar (he had been detained for preaching Christianity), that Caesar is not lord, but Jesus is the supreme ruler of the universe. This was a dangerous and subversive political statement.

For Jews there was only one Lord – God himself. Yet Paul, who was also a Jew, a religious leader (Pharisee) and radical monotheist, takes the idea of 'Lord' and applies it to Jesus. By this statement, Paul is thus effectively declaring that Jesus is God. In other words, Jesus was God before he came to earth,[10] and has now returned to his place with his Father, ruling over all eternity. It is from this existence that Jesus will return.

The Time of the Return

In light of New Testament predictions about the return of Christ, there has been endless speculation about when the return will occur. At the end of the first millennium, for example, there was huge conjecture that the end was about to come.[11] Many people sold their belongings and climbed mountains believing that Jesus was about to return. They were sadly disappointed.

At other points in history, certain world events have led people to believe that the 'end is nigh'. The Jehovah's Witness movement, for example, has given many failed predictions about the return of Jesus.[12] The greatest speculation in recent times revolves around the reconstitution of the nation of Israel in 1948. There have been floods of literature since then suggesting that the world as we know it will soon end. One example is Hal Lindsay's *The Late Great Planet Earth* in 1970. Another example is a book by Dr Stephen Swihart called *Armageddon 198?* which anticipated a final world war and Jesus' return to occur in the 1980s.[13] Clearly he was mistaken. These books suggest that Jesus will return within 40 years or so of 1948 (or 1967 – another important date in the nationhood of Israel). During the Iraq War in the early 1990s some believed that we were witnessing the beginning of WW3, which would trigger the end of the world.

Despite all the speculation, Jesus himself refused to be specific about when the end would come. He said this: 'no one knows about that day or hour, not even the angels in heaven, nor the Son, but only the Father.'[14] He then went on to say that his return would be sudden and unexpected, just as the flood came unexpectedly upon the earth in the days of Noah.[15] In other words, most of the general populace will not unexpected it. However, his people should be ready.

Signs of the Return[16]

While Jesus would not give us a specific date concerning the end, he certainly indicated that certain signs would give us an expectation of his return. He encouraged us that, just as a person in the Middle East can tell that summer is near when they notice that the leaves of a fig tree are tender, we can know that the second coming of Christ is near by the fulfilment of these signs.[17]

In one of Jesus' last discussions with his disciples, he described a set of signs that will accompany his return. He does this in response to a question from his disciples: 'tell us when will this happen, and what will be the sign of your coming and of the end of the age?' Here are the signs he outlines:[18]

Birth Pains. The first set of signs he describes will be like the birth pains of a woman in labour – just as a woman's birth pains increase in intensity as the birth approaches, so there will be a series of events with great intensity before Jesus' return. These include war, famines, earthquakes, persecution, pestilences, false religion, increasing wickedness and decreased love.[19]

It is arguable that we have in fact seen an increase in the intensity and impact of war (e.g. WW1 and WW2). This is also possibly true concerning famine. A few argue too that there has been a continual increase in the number of recorded earthquakes since the 16th century or at the end of the 20th century.[20] It is also possible as we consider the other signs such as intensifying Christian persecution (especially in many Islamic and communist contexts), plagues (AIDS, Ebola, influenza) and a proliferation of religions (see below). Whether or not Jesus has this increasing intensity in mind, he tells us that such events are signs of his coming return.

The Gospel Preached to all Nations. Another key sign Jesus referred to is that the Christian message will be preached to all nations.[21] In other words, when the gospel has been proclaimed in every nation, Jesus will return. We can probably define 'nation' here to mean an ethno-linguistic people group – that is, a clearly defined group of people of common language and culture. Jesus appears to be saying that each must hear the Christian message before the end will come. As a result of this sign, and other appeals of Jesus to preach the gospel, many Christians have devoted their lives and ministries to the completion of this task.

It is not fully clear what it means 'that the gospel has been preached' to every nation. It is probably best to take our cue from the ministries of Jesus and Paul. Jesus made this statement after the gospel had been preached to one nation – Israel. At that point he had travelled with his disciples throughout the country preaching in its towns and cities. He had established a community of faith within Israel including the disciples and others who believed in him. The disciples were then commissioned to go and do the same in the rest of the world. They were to preach the gospel throughout the towns and cities of the world, establishing communities of believers in every nation.[22] Later, Paul focussed his mission on the main urban centres of the Greco-Roman world, preaching and establishing churches. He then moved on to other cities. He moved progressively west from Jerusalem, through Asia Minor (Turkey), and onto Greece with plans to go into Rome and Spain.[23] As he progressed westward, he left behind communities of believers in each city charged with the task of continuing the work he had begun in their regions.[24] That being the case, the gospel will be preached to all nations when Christians have gone to all parts of the world to preach the message and establish Christian communities.

Surprisingly, 2000 years later, this task is still not complete. Despite the fact that Christianity is the world's most widespread and popular religion, there are many people groups who have not yet heard the Christian message. In 2009, according to the 'Joshua Project', which works to assess the completion of this mission, there are 16,304 people groups in the world of which 6,652 (40.8%) remain unreached – that is, 2.72 billion (41.0%) out of 6.64 billion people in the world.[25] If this is correct, there is still a lot of work for God's people to do. Taken at face value, it also indicates that the return of Jesus may not be as close as many Christians claim.

Other Signs. There are other signs mentioned:
a. **Antichrist:** Most Christians see this as a terrible opponent of God who will be a leader of global influence and who will oppose God and his people.[26] Modelled after the caesars of the Roman Empire, Paul tells us that there will be a 'rebellion' and this 'man of lawlessness' will be revealed. He will be everything that Jesus is not, opposing God, claiming to be God, performing false miracles and deceiving many people.[27]

b. **Persecution:** Jesus indicated that at the climax of history that there will be a period of terrible persecution (violent discrimination) against Christians throughout the world.[28]
c. **Terrible suffering:** Jesus referred to a time of terrible global suffering – the likes of which the world has never seen.[29]
d. **False religions and figures:** Jesus said that there would be a proliferation of religions and religious figures claiming to know the way to salvation.[30] Many Christians would see some of the fringe and non-orthodox 'Christian' groups such as various cults, Mormons, Jehovah Witnesses and even extreme liberal expressions of the 'Christian' religion in this regard. The spread of Islam, Hinduism, Buddhism and new age religions and philosophies may also be indicators of this.
e. **Signs in the sky:** Jesus said there would be strange signs in the skies involving the darkening of the sun and the moon, and stars falling from the sky.[31] If literal, this could refer to comets, asteroids or perhaps even nuclear weapons. Alternatively, it was not uncommon in ancient thinking for these things to be used as metaphors for a time of violent instability.

Jerusalem Out of Gentile Hands. In Matthew, Mark and Luke's Gospels, Jesus predicts the destruction of Jerusalem at the hands of the Romans – an event which occurred in AD70.[32] This is remarkable because it is generally agreed that Mark's Gospel was written before the event.[33] Jesus then goes on to describe an exile of the Jewish people:[34] 'they will fall by the sword and will be taken as prisoners to all the nations. Jerusalem will be trampled on by the Gentiles until the times of the Gentiles are fulfilled.' Many believe that this prophecy has been remarkably fulfilled in history not only with Jerusalem being sacked by the Romans in AD70, but with the restoration of the nation of Israel in 1948 and when Jerusalem came back into Jewish hands in 1967.

This event has led some Christians to believe that this is a sign that we are near the climax of history – a culmination with Jerusalem as a key setting.[35] Later in the same passage Jesus says, 'I tell you the truth, *this generation* will certainly not pass away until all these things have happened.'[36] Some take this to mean that 'this generation' refers to the generation of those alive at the time of the restoration of Israel (1948/1967). However, a close reading of the text shows that the reference to 'this generation' comes *after the signs in the sky passage* and may not necessarily be connected directly to the restoration of Israel. Hence, it may be a misinterpretation to link these two concepts directly. If so, we are possibly further from the end than some people think, as we are still waiting for the astral signs referred to above.[37]

It is my personal view that the most significant and potentially verifiable sign would be the preaching of the Christian message to every nation in the world. At that point it seems that there will be an escalation of chaos in the world, great persecution, some form of world government under the leadership of a despotic, anti-religious leader, strange astronomical events, and finally into this turmoil, the return of Christ. In light of the fact that we are still some way off having preached the gospel to all nations, we are probably also still some time away from the return of Christ.

Because of the difficulties of interpreting many of the passages that speak about these things, wise Christians agree that it is important to avoid detailed speculation about the end, and that it is safer to speak in generalities, watching the signs, while living with the knowledge that Jesus might return at any moment. The return of Jesus is not fully described in the New Testament so that we can indulge in endless speculations about details and timing; rather, the intention is to encourage us with hope and a determination to live for God in the present so that we will be ready if he comes back today.

What's God Up To…?

The Nature of the Return

The New Testament records that the return of Christ will be a dramatic cosmic event. The signs which have been mentioned above suggest a time of *world-wide turmoil* seen in war and human misery, a world leader who will persecute Christians and people of other faiths, and astral signs.

Luke tells us that Jesus' return will be 'in the clouds', 'with power and great glory'.[38] Paul suggests there will be the sound of a 'loud command, the voice of the archangel, a trumpet call'.[39] Whether or not we take these descriptions literally or figuratively, they indicate that the moment of Christ's return will be a sight and sound to behold, a time of unprecedented excitement. It will be seen and experienced by all those living at the time.

What happens next is not completely clear. Jesus tells us: 'that is how it will be at the coming of the Son of Man. Two men will be in the field; one will be taken and the other left. Two women will be grinding with a hand mill; one will be taken and the other left.'[40] Paul writes, 'for the Lord himself, with a cry of command, with the archangel's call and with the sound of God's trumpet, will descend from heaven, and the dead in Christ will rise first. Then we who are alive, who are left, will be caught up in the clouds together with them to meet the Lord in the air; and so we will be with the Lord forever.'[41]

These words have led some to believe in the concept of the *'rapture'* in which, upon Jesus' return, believers who have died will rise from the grave, and, along with those who are alive, will be taken to meet Jesus in the air, and go with him to heaven. This would mean the remainder of humanity will be *left behind* on earth for some period of time – a time of great suffering called the 'tribulation'. Others (including myself) read these passages differently. They believe those 'left behind' will in fact be the believers and not the unbelievers. Just as Noah and his family were left behind when the flood swept away those who refused to enter the ark that Noah built, so those who reject the Christian message will in some way be 'swept away' by God at Christ's return.

Jesus will return and the dead who have believed in him will be raised to life. Those Christians still living at the time will welcome Jesus to this world where he will establish God's reign completely on earth. He will restore his world to its original intention. This is the new heaven and a new earth described in glorious pictorial language in Isaiah 65-66 and Revelation 21-22. It is, in a sense, the Eden of Genesis 1-2 restored. The world will be healed, evil vanquished, justice established, and eternal life granted to God's people. Indeed, God's work of restoration will be completed. This is God's dream and our hope.

There is also controversy surrounding interpretation of passages that talk about the period after Christ's return. Revelation 20:1-6 speaks of a period of a thousand years in which Christ returns and then reigns on earth leading up to the final eternal destruction of evil. The meaning of this 'millennium' is debated – some see it as a literal 1000 year reign of Christ on earth or as symbolic of a long period of Christ's reign *after* his return ('premillenialism'). Others believe in different ways that the period we are in now is the millennium *before* Christ's return ('amillenialism', 'postmillennialism').[42] Whichever of these views is correct,[43] it is agreed by all Bible-believing Christians that Christ will return and reign over the earth.

As with the questions surrounding the specific time of Jesus' return, we should avoid detailed speculation about the exact nature of what will happen. When we read the different accounts, it is difficult to put them together in a conclusive and coherent manner and to be completely confident of the sequence of events. One of the problems is that the key book in the Bible that deals with the return of Jesus (*Revelation*) is, without doubt, the most difficult book in the New Testament to interpret. This is due to it being 'apocalyptic' literature, containing highly symbolic, metaphoric and poetic language. In addition, putting a timeline together means that we need to somewhat arbitrarily take verses from all over the Bible and link them up. Many Christians (I among them) are wary of such approaches and do not believe the Bible gives us a specific timetable. Rather, it is better to stick to the big picture aspects of the event that the New Testament makes clear. So what are these events?

The Events Surrounding the Return

While the exact detail of the sequence of events is unclear, there are some things we can be confident about concerning the events surrounding the return of Christ:

The Signs Fulfilled. In the lead-up to the coming of Christ, the signs referred to by the New Testament will be fulfilled. As noted above, interpreting these with absolute certainty is difficult; hence, we must be open-minded about the specific details. As I mentioned before, we are watching most of all for the completion of the mission of taking the gospel to every 'nation'. If the interpretation suggested above is correct, this will be the point at which the Christian message has been made known in every language. In addition, when a community of faith is established in every people group, the mission is complete. As this mission is not yet fulfilled, it is probable that we are not there yet or as close as some Christians claim. However, with the speed of communication and ease of travel in today's world, this may be completed quite quickly.

The Actual Return. Jesus returns dramatically in the clouds. Exactly what this will look like is unclear. However, it is presented as if Jesus will appear in earth's atmosphere, be seen by millions, and the events surrounding the end of the world will be set in motion. It will be an unmistakable glorious global event.

The Resurrection of the Dead. At this point there will be a resurrection of the dead. Again this is debated. Some believe that only the believers will rise and others will not. Most believe that all will rise including believers and unbelievers and all humanity will stand in judgment before God.[44] What matters for us is that God will raise to eternal life those who respond to the good news of Jesus.

The Judgment of All Humanity. All humanity will be gathered in some way before God and will be judged on the basis of what they have said and done.[45] This can sound like a fearful event. For those who have believed in Jesus, this is not to be feared. Rather, it is a joyful time when God's faithful receive eternal life.

Eternal Life for the Faithful. Those who believe in God, having a personal relationship with him as originally intended, are granted eternal life with him. The Bible is not explicit about what will happen to those who have not heard the Christian message or die before the age of comprehension. However, there are clues to suggest that those who lived before Christ or have not heard the message will be *saved by their faith in God as they perceived him in creation and common human morality.*[46] Those who were mentally unable to comprehend God or died as children will most likely be saved by a gracious God. God's people will be with God forever. The Bible speaks of a new heaven and a new earth which merge into one and in which God will dwell with his people.[47] It is debated whether this will be in another completely new place or dimension separate from this universe (heaven) or, as I have suggested above, it will be *this world restored* after it has been purified. The Bible is not completely clear on this – some verses point towards a renewed earth and others to a completely new dimension.[48]

Either way the Bible is explicit – God will live with humanity forever as he intended in the beginning, in a new creation of wonder, creativity, excitement and evil-free purity.[49] Popular misconceptions of eternal boredom, playing a harp on a cloud, could not be further from the truth. The Bible anticipates a place of unprecedented excitement, creativity and thrill – a world and universe of beauty to be explored and experienced to the full.

While we cannot fully anticipate what a new or renewed earth will be like, we can use our imaginations. Imagine what it might be like to live eternally with the being who made this universe and world. Imagine what creativity we will see. We could explore the universe. But why would we limit our thinking to this universe or dimension? There may be multiple dimensions and universes for us to explore. We will be incorruptible and immortal and have access to immense unprecedented creativity. We will have many of our human limitations and fears removed. What a glorious experience it will be as we explore the fullness of God's glorious creativity.

Eternal Destruction for the Rest. Those who have rejected a personal relationship with God are consigned to eternal destruction, separated from God forever.[50] The nature of this destruction is debated. There are three essential views. Traditional Christianity has believed that all humanity from their birth will live on indefinitely (the immortality of the soul) either in heaven or hell. Hell is consistently referred to as a place of burning. The traditional view is that these references to 'burning' and 'flames' are to be taken literally. As such, hell is a place in which evil, including Satan himself and all unsaved sinners, will be confined and burn eternally in great pain (yet without being consumed). It is a place of punishment for evil.

A number of Christians, however, believe that the references to 'burning' should be read figuratively and point not to literal burning, but to a place of separation from God and all that is good. If so, we are still talking about a dimension of unimaginable misery and loneliness, if not literal fire.[51]

Others believe that only those who have a saving relationship with God will receive eternal life and others will be extinguished. They believe that the concept of an immortal soul is not found in the New Testament and that resurrection is conditional on faith. This interpretation means that only those who believe in God will be raised from the dead. The remainder of humanity are extinguished or simply remain deceased.

Hell, then, is a place of literal burning or some other means of destruction; alternatively it is symbolic of all evil including Satan and unsaved humanity being extinguished forever.[52]

Whichever view is correct, this everlasting separation from God is unimaginably horrible and to be avoided at all costs. As we saw in chapter two, all people participate in evil (i.e. are sinners) and must be saved to avoid being destroyed or eternally separated along with all that is evil. This destruction, or confining of evil, is essential for the ultimate eternal goodness of the cosmos – that is, if evil is allowed to live on, its destructive force will continue to cause chaos eternally. Evil is an affront to God and must be removed – it would be unjust not to do so. Hell ensures that ultimately, good will prevail.

Removing evil is also an act of mercy for the people who have chosen to follow God. Hell, in whatever form, pays respect to the choices of humanity. Those who do not wish to spend eternity with God are granted their request – they are irrevocably separated from him. As such, God honours the individual's choice completely – albeit reluctantly, for he wants all to be saved.

Hence, while it may appear that hell is a difficult and unfair concept, when understood from the perspective of love, eternity and purity, hell is fair, loving and just. It is required due to the mercy and justice of God, and so that good will prevail.

Be Ready

When Jesus spoke about his return, he followed it up with a series of instructions and parables telling people to be ready. He said:

> *Keep awake* therefore, for you do not know on what day your Lord is coming. But understand this: if the owner of the house had known in what part of the night the thief was coming, he would have stayed awake and would not have let his house be broken into. Therefore you also *must be ready*, for the Son of Man is coming at an *unexpected hour*.[53]

In other words, we can try and read the signs, but we need to be ready at all times – he is going to come when many people least expect it.

Jesus told us how to be ready. He taught that we should be like a good worker who is left in charge of a business by the boss and is found to have looked after the business well when the boss returns home.[54] He also taught that we are to invest the wonderful things God has given us not for our own personal gain, but for his kingdom and the good of humanity (i.e. as part of God's great project).[55] Furthermore, he taught that we are ready if we are generous to those in need – in particular the poor, immigrants and other strangers, the sick and those in prison.[56]

In other words, we are ready if we respond to Jesus as God wants us to respond to him. Our readiness for the return of Jesus depends on our response to Jesus and his message.

Conclusion

The answer to the question 'How will it end?' is that it will end when the message about Jesus has gone to all corners of the world. After a time of crisis, Jesus will return. He will return in a blaze of glory. Evil will be vanquished. God's people will be with him forever. We are challenged by Jesus to be prepared for this glorious climax to history. To be ready we must respond to the message. So now we turn to the final chapter of this discussion. What should our response be to the message we have heard about God?

Questions For Reflection

1. Which makes more sense to you? That God will come and destroy this world and recreate a new one? Or that God will restore this one?
2. Do you think we are near the return of Christ? How should we live either way?
3. What signs of Christ's return intrigue you?
4. How do we avoid too much speculation concerning Christ's return, yet also prepare for it?
5. Do you think the explanation for the notion of eternal destruction is reasonable in light of God's love, justice and purposes?
6. What do you think the return of Christ might be like?
7. How can we be ready for Christ's return?

FIVE
RESPONSE

So we come to a very important part of what God is up to on planet earth. Thus far we have found that:

a. We are each made for an eternal personal *relationship* with God.
b. There has been a terrible *rupture* in this relationship caused by the human choice to sin and so participate in evil, which causes us to be separated from God, human relationships to be fractured and creation itself to be damaged. The only hope for humanity and God's world is divine salvation.
c. God, due to his love and mercy, has moved to effect the *restoration* of the initial relationship and the whole world through sending his son Jesus to die and rise again to save people, the world and all creation.
d. There is a great and glorious day coming when this same Jesus will *return* and the world as we know it will come to its climax. There will be a judgement, and each will be granted either eternal life with God as he originally intended in a new or renewed earth, or eternal destruction and separation from him.

So it is plain to see what the gospel is all about, at least in these broad strokes. But how do we get saved by this gospel? As the Philippian jailor said to the Apostle Paul in the prison in Philippi, 'What must I do to be saved?'[1]

What is the Right Response?

The New Testament tells us that, while it is God's will that all are saved,[2] not all will be saved.[3] This brings us to the fifth and final R: *'response'*. That is, if God wants us to spend eternity with him and Jesus has come to save us to ensure we do, what do we have to do to be saved through the cross and resurrection? As we look into the New Testament we see that there is one type of response that saves, but the different writers have various ways of expressing this response.

Repent and Follow Totally

When Jesus addressed the question of human response he talked about three aspects. First, he used the term *'repent'*. Right at the beginning of his ministry he called people to 'repent, for the Kingdom of God is near.'[4] He called for this response throughout his ministry.[5] He said explicitly that the reason he came was 'to call sinners to repentance',[6] and he sent his disciples to preach with the aim of people repenting as a result.[7] So what did Jesus mean by 'repenting'?

Our word 'repent' comes from the Latin root for 'penitent'. This indicates one sense of the word 'repent' – 'to feel regret, sorrow or contrition' for doing wrong.

However, this does not entirely cover what Jesus had in mind. The Greek verb is *metanoeō* (noun = *metanoia*) which means to change (*meta*) one's mind (cf. *nous*) – that is, a 'total change, both in thought and behaviour, with respect to how one should both think and act'.[8] From Jesus' mouth, then, it means turning from a life that is devoted to one's selfish desires.

Another way of putting this is to think about Jesus as King or Lord. Jesus is the supreme ruler of the universe. He is the emperor, the boss, the leader, the ruler of all. To respond appropriately to such a being is to give total allegiance to the ruler, bowing the knee in complete submission.

That being the case, the right response of someone wanting salvation in Christ is to prioritise their devotion to God and his purposes above all other allegiances. In other words, we put him above things like business, money, a husband or a wife, one's own family, a love of sport, a love of pleasure, sexual lust, a passion for fast cars or whatever. Some of these things in and of themselves are not wrong – in fact many are very good things – but, when they are given greater priority than God, they take our focus away from where it should really be.

In my own case, to repent meant turning away from an unhealthy love of sport and desire for prestige and pleasure, and instead living for God. Turning to God does not mean neglecting your spouse, family or the responsibility of making a living; rather it means putting God in the driver's seat of your life and allowing him to direct your steps. In fact he will lead people to be more committed than ever to their spouses, families, businesses, and even to sport or art, but only in second place to their commitment to the Lord of the universe.

A second concept Jesus uses is encapsulated in the word *'follow'*. Repentance can seem like a static concept whereas to 'follow' means that once we have turned from our own direction, we keep moving in the footsteps of Jesus. Jesus often spoke of following. He said to the first disciples by the Sea of Galilee, 'come *follow* me and I will make you fishers of people'.[9] He said it to Levi (Matthew) the tax collector: '*follow* me!'[10] He said it to the rich young ruler: 'go, sell your possessions, and give the money to the poor and you will have treasure in heaven; then *follow* me.'[11] So the right response is to follow Jesus. Of course, this does not mean living exactly as he did as a first-century Jew – rather, it means living according to the pattern he laid down for humanity: faith, love, hope and goodness.

An important aspect of following is the idea of *total commitment* – full-on following. There are no half-measures in Jesus' appeal. We hear this in his declaration, 'seek first the kingdom of God and his righteousness' – that is, seek it *before anything else*,[12] as first priority.

Following Jesus will inevitably involve struggle and suffering. On another occasion Jesus said, 'if anyone would come after me, they must deny themselves and *take up their cross daily* and follow me.'[13] This calls to mind the crucifixion when Jesus carried his cross along the *Via Dolorosa* (the road to his place of execution) in great torment. It speaks to us of following through great difficulties, perhaps even to the point of death if need be. Jesus goes on to explain that this type of following is a denial of self for the sake of the mission: 'for whoever wants to save their life will lose it, but whoever loses their life for me will save it. What good is it for anyone to gain the whole world, and yet lose or forfeit their very self?'[14] This carries a warning: if we seek to preserve our own life we will lose it. If we give our life over to Jesus and his purposes, we will gain it – we will live forever in a relationship with God.

In other words, the response Jesus looked for was *total repentance and wholehearted following*. In keeping with the concept of following, Jesus describes the Christian life as a journey. Jesus says, 'enter through the narrow gate; for the gate is wide and the road is easy that leads to destruction, and there are many who take it. For the gate is narrow and the road is hard that leads to life, and there are few who find it.'[15] This tells us something about the nature of following. It is challenging, and the clause 'few who find it' implies that most will not take that road. We are to walk the entire journey to be saved. Jesus later reiterates this stating: 'only he/she who holds firm to the end will be saved'.[16]

The cost of following is well worth it for the many glorious rewards promised to us. First, there is the honour of being a follower of the creator of the universe. Secondly, there is the peace that God gives us, even when we go through great struggles. We know that 'all things work for the good of those who love Him, and are called according to his purpose.'[17] Thirdly, God dwells within us by his Spirit; we do not walk alone, but we have God's Spirit in us, impelling us, comforting us, strengthening us, leading us and generally giving us the glorious experience of being filled with God. Fourthly, there is the reward of being part of God's people. We live our lives knowing with absolute confidence that we are friends and family with God. We are brothers and sisters. We are not alone no matter what we face. Wherever we go, we have a great sense of solidarity and support. Fifthly, we are invited by the creator of the universe to join him in his 'cosmission' – his great restoration project. We are granted the privilege of being called and commissioned by the King of the world to help him restore it to his original dream. What an honour!

And finally, and most significantly, there is the ultimate reward God promises all who are faithful to the end – the wonders of eternal life. At this time, all suffering will end, our tears will be wiped away, our bodies restored, all injustice and inequality will be gone, death overcome and our freedom total. Let your imagination go and envisage this world as it could be – you, eternally alive, God's presence with you, and the joy of unlimited opportunity and creativity!

So, one concept describing the right way to respond to Jesus is *'to repent' and 'to follow' with all our being*. This is not an appeal for perfection, but for a commitment to follow Jesus through thick and thin.

To Believe the Gospel and to Live Out that Faith

Throughout most of the New Testament, especially in the writings of

John and Paul, the concept that encapsulates the right response to God is 'to believe' – that is, to 'have faith'.

For example, John writes, 'yet to all who received him, to those who *believed* in his name, he gave the right to become children of God – children born not of natural descent, nor of human decision or a husband's will, but born of God.'[18] Here the relationship with God is established through receiving Jesus and '*believing* in his name'. One of the verses that best captures this is Jesus' statement in John 3:16, 'For God so loved the world that he gave his one and only Son, that whoever *believes in him* shall not perish but have eternal life.' Similarly he says, 'whoever *believes in the Son* has eternal life, but whoever rejects the Son will not see life, for God's wrath remains on them.'[19]

Paul uses the same term, 'faith or belief', with regard to the Christian response. For example he says, 'this righteousness from God comes through *faith* in Jesus Christ to all who *believe*.'[20] And again he writes, 'for by grace you have been saved *through faith*, and this is not your own doing; it is the gift of God – not the result of works, so that no one may boast.'[21] Here, the right response to God's gift of salvation is faith.[22]

So What is this Faith that Saves?

In my understanding of Paul and the other New Testament writers, the response that saves involves two *simultaneous* internal instant dynamics: an *initial acceptance of the message* along with *an intentional ongoing life commitment to Christ*.

An Initial Acceptance of the Message. First, it involves an initial acceptance of the message of Christ as *the* truth. This means that we hear that Christ has died to save us and *believe in Christ as Saviour*.

Response

In Paul's mind this happens when we hear the Christian message and believe it. A good example of this is when he reminds the Christians in Ephesus about the moment of their salvation. He says, 'and you also were included in Christ when you *heard the word of truth*, the *gospel* of your salvation. Having *believed*, you were marked in him with a seal, the promised Holy Spirit, who is a deposit guaranteeing our inheritance until the redemption of those who are God's possession – to the praise of his glory.'[23]

In these verses Paul explains *the process of initial salvation*:

a. A person hears (or reads as in this book) the Christian message (the gospel).
b. That person accepts it as truth (i.e. he/she believes it).
c. He/she instantly receives the Spirit of God (i.e. that person enters into relationship with God).

On another occasion Paul explains that 'faith comes through hearing the message and the message is heard through the word of Christ.'[24] That is, the point at which believing faith takes root in a person's life is usually at the moment that they hear the message and accept it as truth.[25]

Many (like my own children) who are brought up as Christians, do not remember this 'moment of decision'. However, there will have been points during their journey when they made a conscious decision to walk with Christ. Others, who were converted out of a non-religious life, will vividly remember the moment of their conversion. I certainly do. As I briefly mentioned in the introduction, I was 13 years old from a family with little active belief in Christ. A Christian man named Brian Chitty carefully explained the Christian message to me at an after-school club in Rarotonga. As I heard the message internally I found myself believing it. Unfortunately I did not follow through on this first glimpse of faith and quickly returned to my life of self-centred sin. Yet it was as if a seed had been planted in my soul waiting to come to life.[26] The process was completed eleven years later when God drew me back to him and I made an ongoing commitment to live for God forever.

An Intentional Ongoing Life Commitment. The second key factor in salvation faith is 'an intentional ongoing life commitment'. The kind of faith that saves you involves more than an initial one-off mental acceptance of a truth (although that is how it always begins). It is more than saying, 'I believe that!' It involves simultaneously resolving to live out life on the basis of this faith, acting on the new belief and responding to it with our attitudes, words and actions. Put another way, it means believing in Jesus not only as our saviour, but also as *Lord*. It means *trusting* him – giving our lives over to his leadership. It involves a shift from an allegiance to our own selfish ambitions, to an allegiance to the things of God. It means realising what a glorious thing God has done for us by creating us, reaching out to us, saving us and wanting to spend eternity with us. So much so, that we want to respond by loving him back and serving him with our lives.

Imagine you are at the airport waiting to fly to Australia and your flight is delayed. You are annoyed but as you sit there waiting, someone comes up and asks your name. You tell them who you are and they say, 'Come with me, we have a special flight for you to Australia.' You say, 'What?' They say that the airline is sorry for the delay and have arranged a special flight *just for you* which will be leaving in five minutes. You then have a choice: do you believe them or not? You decide it is true and walk with the person to the plane. As you stand outside the plane alone on the tarmac you have the choice of following through on the belief or walking away.

In reality, if you do not board the plane you do not truly believe. You only truly believe if you board the plane. In terms of faith then, true faith means believing that Jesus will save us or, in terms of this analogy, boarding the plane to take that journey with him in the pilot's seat. It means trusting him as the pilot of your life. Incidentally, if you got on the plane, you would find there are many already on it. There are many who, like me, have trusted the pilot and found that he is perfectly trustworthy and faithful.

So believing faith accepts Jesus as Saviour and involves an intention to live for him as Lord.

This does not mean we will succeed in living a perfect life or that we are able to *do* anything to save ourselves. As we noted near the beginning of this book, we cannot live a perfect life, no matter how hard we try. That's the point of Christianity – we rely utterly on Jesus to save us. We are not saved by any human effort. Christian thinkers state it like this: we are not saved by any works or human merit, but we are saved by grace – God's gift through Jesus who died for us on the cross. We are saved by his mercy and his mercy alone. Our positive response is the only thing God wants from us.

You see, no matter how hard we try, once we accept Jesus as Lord, we will not always honour him as our Lord, despite our best intentions. We will fail to live up to the standards of God and his kingdom. That is why Paul goes out of his way to say that we are *not saved by works*, but by grace, through our response of faith.[27] But if we continue to be committed to God we remain in his love, despite our failings.

We seek to do good and please God because we realise who he is and what he has done for us. We are motivated by his love to do good for others.[28] As the full significance of the love of Christ becomes real to us, we cannot help but want to serve him out of gratitude for all he has done.[29] That God wants us to do good is evident in the verse that follows

Paul's words above: 'for we are God's workmanship, created in Christ Jesus *to do good works*, which God prepared in advance for us to do.'[30] This shows that while we are in no way saved by good works, we will go on to do good works once we are saved.

In the end, then, it all comes down to *sincere intention*. We believe and set out on a journey *intending* to live for God with all our being. We stumble and fall, we have good days and bad days and we make mistakes along the way. But none of these separate us from God if we retain that central belief in Jesus as our saviour and keep living with the intention of honouring Jesus as Lord.

A good example of this from the Bible is Abraham.[31] Paul describes Abraham as a model of faith who believed God. Because of his belief, Abraham's faith was credited to him as righteousness – that is, he was saved on the basis of his faith.[32] If we read the accounts of Abraham from Genesis chapters 12 to 25 we see that he was a good but flawed man. At times he wavered in his belief, he was dishonest and he looked for ways to hurry up the fulfilment of God's promises to him.[33] Yet, overall, although he had moments of doubt and struggle, he retained an underlying trust in God's promise and a commitment to follow him in obedience.[34] As such, he is called the father of all who believe.

Then What Happens?

This is the amazing thing about the Christian message. All we have to do is say 'yes' to God's offer of salvation and resolve to make Jesus the most important priority of our lives. Admittedly, though, some would see this as an extremely high price, as they value the idea of complete control over their own existence. I recently heard the story of one such person, who while convinced of the Christian message, refused to, as he put it, 'sign my life away' to God.

However, when we consider what God has done for us, giving ourselves to him is nothing in comparison! After all, he created our world for us, he gave us life, he governs history limiting the power of evil and moving it toward its climax. He has provided for us – the wonder of flora and fauna all placed here for us to experience and enjoy. And supremely – although we have all rejected him, done our own thing and contributed to the brokenness of his world – he sent his son Jesus to save us. Although we are prone to wrongdoing and do not really deserve to be with God, he is so determined to be with us that he gave his son to die for us. And he did it in such a way that he still gives us the freedom to accept or reject him.

When we accept him he promises to begin that life of relationship straight away! When we say yes to his offer and resolve to live for him, he instantaneously sends his Spirit, his personal presence, into our hearts to transform us. By his Spirit he dwells in our lives and restores us progressively. He gently changes our attitudes, our actions and words to be more and more in keeping with his character and will. We are not instantly made perfect, although many who become Christians do experience an immediate difference.

He gives us a reason to live, a renewed purpose. Whereas before we may have felt despair, we now see his glory in the world. We understand the world in a new way and have a fresh resolve to participate in its transformation. He takes our natural talents, our experiences (bad and good) and, as he restores us, he leads us to use these things in a way that benefits the world. We are invited to join his great project of cosmic transformation, of restoring the world to his original intention and human society as it was always meant to be. By his Spirit he gives us new gifts as he chooses, spiritual ones, some of which will be supernatural, enabling us to do things like heal the sick, preach the gospel, to know his plans and so on.[35]

So he not only saves us, but he also invites us to join his team of cosmic transformers – he calls us into his service, to work in his 'cosmission'. He will take us as we are with all our talents, our weaknesses, our experiences and he will send us out into his world to be his agents of transformation. He wants us to join his team and work with him to see every living being experience all that he has for them and to live with him forever in eternity. He will progressively repair our internal brokenness – the things in our past that have hurt us – he will transform us into the people he intended us to be.

He will send us out into our workplaces, our families, our social networks, into all parts of human society, and through our skills and talents make the world a better place. All we have to do is accept his offer of salvation and resolve to walk with him through life. He will protect us, provide for us, lead us, restore us and inspire us. Not that our lives will suddenly become perfect and we will no longer suffer in this world as some teach. No, like Christ and Paul, we will face enormous challenges as we seek to bring God's message and goodness to the world. But the experience of Christians through the ages is that God will often intervene into our situations and we will experience a miracle. At other times God will choose not to intervene directly with deliverance or healing but will walk with us through our suffering and his glory will be seen in our weakness. His Spirit will empower and sustain us in suffering. Either way, God will be with us and life will be so much more worth living.

My Story

The message in this book is more that just theory or theology to me. In my own life I have experienced God. Before I fully accepted Jesus as my Saviour and Lord, I was thoroughly disillusioned with the world. I recognised the world was ruptured and broken, but couldn't see the light that was shining in it. My life revolved around trying to gain prestige on the rugby and cricket fields, and partying off-field. I struggled through university and then dropped out with an incomplete BA degree. I was living with my girlfriend in a de-facto relationship, and somehow got accepted into teachers training college. Outwardly, I may have appeared to be an impressive and talented young man, but inwardly I did not have it together at all! I could see that the world was in serious trouble with nuclear threats, materialism, increasing rebellion, violence and family disintegration. It seemed to me that the world was full of greed; selfishness reigned and the world was en-route to destruction.

After months of internal struggle and angst, I realised that the way the Bible viewed the world was true – it is governed by evil, greed and futility. I also recalled the gospel message I had heard in Rarotonga when I was 13. I remembered that Brian Chitty had told me that if I believed in Jesus as Saviour and Lord, and if I repented and followed him, I would be saved. So on New Years Day 1985, at age 24, I again surrendered my life to God. I accepted Jesus as my saviour and Lord, and I resolved to live for him forever. I was determined to live as a disciple (learner) of Jesus.

I cannot adequately describe to you the wonderful experience this journey was and has been to this day. Instantly I experienced a new internal power to begin to change my life. My outlook on life was transformed. I gave up my addiction to alcohol and recreational drugs. I joined a church and explored my faith with new friends. My girlfriend Emma also became a Christian and, after marrying that same year, we embarked on the most amazing journey following Jesus. She has gone from remedial reader and party animal to Presbyterian minister! I have gone from university dropout to Doctor in Theology, holding a position as a lecturer in New Testament studies, currently at Laidlaw College in Auckland, New Zealand.

Along the journey God has at times provided for us miraculously. Progressively he is healing our broken self-esteems and bit-by-bit he is restoring and maturing us, leading us to the full potential he has for us as we serve him. We still experience suffering, the decay of aging, the struggles of bodies battered and bruised by life, but inwardly we are being continually renewed. We remain flawed with human weaknesses, but he has given us forgiveness and continues to work in and through us. He has given us three wonderful daughters who have grown up loving him and experiencing his grace.

It is the greatest honour in the universe to be at the service of our creator God whose handiwork is all around us. When we have hit hard times (as you do), he has been there giving us meaning and restoring us. He is a wonderful God, well worth following.

I have seen him perform miracles. I have seen him on a few occasions heal the deaf and injured, and restore the broken-hearted. I have also seen many situations where God has not intervened to physically heal someone with great physical challenges, and yet in the lives of such people I have seen the greatness of faith, triumph over adversity, glory through suffering – all empowered by God. In fact, it is in the lives of such people that I have seen the greatest faith, as they walk triumphantly with God's strength despite their seeming weakness. I have seen him comfort the lost and turn people around from futility to purpose, from sin to purity and despair to hope.

The greatest thing of all is the assurance of living with him forever. All we have to do is hang in there, following, and we will be with him forever in the world to come without tears, suffering, pain, torment, war and famine. Indeed, when we feel that we cannot go on, he steps in every time – 'he will bring to completion the good work he began in us.'[36]

Response

What About You?

This brings us to the ultimate question – what about you? The faith that saves starts from the point of believing the good news. Having heard this explanation of it, do you accept it as truth? Do you believe the gospel? That is, do you believe that you were created to have an eternal relationship with God? Do you accept that you are separated from him because of your complicit participation in evil (i.e. sin)? Do you accept too that the world of human relationships and creation is fragmented by this same problem?

Do you accept that the only way to be saved is through Jesus who died on the cross in your place to take upon himself the consequences of your sin? Do you accept his free offer of salvation? Are you willing to make allegiance to him and his ways the number one allegiance of your life? Do you yearn for the world to be as God dreamed and want to work with him as an agent of transformation in his great project?

You don't have to know all the answers, but if your answer to Jesus is 'yes', it is pretty simple from here. Just go ahead and tell God yourself. This may feel strange – prayer is kind of weird when you start out. But he is listening, waiting for this prayer, and he will hear you in the deep silence of his universe where he dwells in all places at all times. After telling him, simply trust him and he guarantees you his salvation! He will instantly enter your life by his Spirit, his own personal presence, and together you and he will go on a great adventure. You may actually have a physical or emotional response to this moment, may feel your heart 'strangely warmed', or nothing much may happen. Don't be fazed either way – God *promises* to dwell in you. Over time, you will see the signs of him in your life. He will be seen in the little things: fresh attitudes, a new outlook, a renewed desire for God, goodness and love. He will take all that you are and have been – the good, the bad and the ugly – and, like a potter moulds clay on a wheel, will shape you into everything you were created to be.

Actually, he will make you into something far better – he knows you better than you know yourself, and you can trust him to lead you to great places. I'm not saying that life will necessarily be better or easier or that all your problems will be instantly resolved. As I have mentioned, the experience of many people is that life as a Christian is a constant challenge. This is especially so where Christianity is despised and where people are psychologically, politically and physically persecuted like the first Christians were. However, while your circumstances may be tough, inwardly you will have a new set of resources to cope with the challenges. You will find the deepest meaning in your faith by facing difficulties, because you will see God at work and will experience his strength in your weakness.

You will become a part of a great cosmic project of restoring God's world. What a great call and challenge! He will take you as you are in that part of the world where you live, and he and you will get to work with all his power and resources to reverse the ravages of evil and sin.

So, now all that is left is for you to make a decision. You do not need to make that choice right now. You can go away and think about it. But I would urge you to think it through and resolve to follow Jesus as your saviour and Lord. We never know what tomorrow will bring. Those in the Twin Towers on September 11, 2001 or before the Tsunami in Asia on Boxing Day, 2004 or the Haitian earthquake in 2010 had no idea what was about to happen – neither do we.

You may be thinking, 'But what do I do if I don't believe this account of God and Jesus?' or are simply not sure. If you find all this too unbelievable and really can't accept the existence of God, I encourage you to speak out into the great unknown, the void, and say something like this: 'God, if you are for real and truly exist, please reveal yourself to me. If you want a relationship with me, make yourself known so I can see you are real and follow you to the salvation that Christians talk about.' I am sure that if you do, he will make himself known. Over time his existence will become more evident in your life, because he wants to have a friendship with you.

I remember saying something like this to the great unknown when I was in the midst of disillusionment and futility – and God responded. I cannot tell you exactly what happened except that it was like my 'blindness' lifted and one day as I was looking out at a beautiful view, I realised there was a God. All that you need is to be open to the possibility.

If you have read this book and really want to follow Jesus, I encourage you, where you are right now, to pray to him. Express how you feel to him – he will hear your words and emotions. You might use this prayer:

Dear God,
Thank you for this message of salvation. I get what you are up to. I want to live in an everlasting relationship with you. I am sorry for all the wrong things I have done that have ruptured the relationship you want to have with me. Thank you for sending Jesus to restore that relationship. I ask that you will save me through your death and resurrection. I resolve that from this time on, as best I can, I will seek to honour you and obey you with my life. I believe in Jesus, I believe in your salvation. When I die, or you return, whichever comes first, please take me to be with you forever in your Kingdom. I accept your offer of salvation and I resolve to follow you and live for you as my Lord. Please send your Spirit into my being to transform me, guide me and make me into the person you want me to be. May I be a part of your great restoration of your world? Thank you for your salvation… Amen.

If you prayed that prayer with conviction, you are now accepted into an eternal relationship with God through Jesus. He has sent his Spirit into your heart. You are his child!

Questions for Reflection

1. What word for response do you find the most meaningful? Follow? Repent? Believe?
2. What does it mean to believe in Jesus?
3. What do you think it might mean to have God's Spirit living in your being?
4. What is your story? How would you describe your experience of God?

So, what happens next?

SIX
WHERE TO FROM HERE?

If you have got this far, I sincerely thank you for taking the time to consider this message. If you prayed the prayer above with a genuine heart, congratulations! You have just made the whole purpose of this book worthwhile. The Bible says that heaven celebrates every time someone turns to God.[1] He has heard your prayer and you are now able to say, 'I am saved.' He guarantees that he will save you as you continue to walk with him by faith, and that he will never leave your side.[2]

As I have said, this life of faith is a relationship and a journey. So here are some things that can help you get going on your journey as you follow Jesus.

Learn the Story

First, I encourage you to get a Bible and begin to read it to learn what it means to follow God. The Bible is God's message to us and it is our main source of knowledge about him. It is his story – a great story – telling of creation, the fall, his program of restoration through the history of Israel culminating in Jesus, the great mission of restoration, the return of Jesus and eternity living with God. As you read it the Holy Spirit, who is now within you, will bring the words alive in a totally new way.

I recommend you begin by re-reading this book, and check out the verses in the endnotes as you go so that you fully understand the message. It is good to memorise the verses that really resonate with you.

What's God Up To…?

In the Bible, begin by reading through the accounts of Jesus found in Matthew, Mark, Luke and John. Jesus is the heart of the Christian faith and these stories about Jesus are the heart of the Bible. Once you have done that, read through the rest of the New Testament taking a note of how the story unfolds, who God (Father, Son and the Spirit) is, and how we should live. Then I encourage you to go back to the beginning of the Bible and read the whole story of the Old Testament. Before you do, read chapters 7 and 13 in the New Testament book of Acts, and the book of Hebrews, which helps make sense of the Old Testament.

As you read your Bible, note down what the Father, Jesus and the Spirit are like and think about how God wants us to live – then seek to live like that. It is good to spend a little time every day reading the Bible – it is like our road map, our manual for living.

Pray Every Day

Secondly, start talking to God – he is always with you. We call this prayer. Pray as much as you can, throughout the day, about everything in your life – your family, this nation, the world. Don't be shy to pray for your own needs at work, sport or whatever you do. God is interested in everything in your life. He is not only concerned about what we label as the *spiritual* stuff. He is concerned about *everything* in his world. He is concerned about you, your work, your sport, your hobbies, your family, your interests and all that makes us human. He delights in you and wants to bless you.

He has promised that when we ask him he will listen and respond. He doesn't always answer our prayers exactly the way we expect because he is God and he knows best. But he always responds and his answers are always the best for us and his world, even if we do not always see it at the time.

Remember though, while it is good to pray for our own needs, we should not be self-centred in prayer. Christianity is about love and having concern for the needs of others. It is about putting others first. So pray for others as well. Pray for those who are ill and for those facing struggles in their lives – pray that they too can become Christians if they are not already. Pray for the world and all its problems. Pray for God's great project – that every corner of the world will reflect his glory and be as he intended it to be. It is good to learn the 'Lord's Prayer' off by heart and make it the basis for your prayer life. Jesus gave it to us to be prayed everyday with a sincere heart.[3]

Live to Please God, Trust God, Love Him and Others

Thirdly, seek to please God with your life. As you read the Bible, pray and learn more about him, you will become aware of things you should do and things in your life that need to be changed. As these things come to light, make the changes you sense God is calling you to. Always remember what God has done for you and how glorious he and his story are – try to honour him with your life. But remember God doesn't want us to get all uptight about this – he wants us to experience freedom, joy and hope. Be careful not to lose hope if you slip up and fail, no matter how badly. His forgiveness is limitless. If you do mess up, ask his forgiveness with a sincere heart, learn the lesson, and move on, seeking to do better next time. No matter how far you fall, what sins you commit, he will take you back if you come to him with a genuine heart, seeking his forgiveness.[4] In fact, were you to spend every minute of your life in rebellion against God and in the last moment, genuinely turned to him, he would take you warts and all and spend eternity with you![5]

Above all, trust God in everything. If things look bleak as they sometimes are, remember that God is with you and he will lead you through. The realities of life, its struggles and suffering will still challenge us, but

God will be there with us as we face them. Sometimes he will intervene and do an obvious miracle, other times he will not – either way, he will bring you through!

And equally importantly, love others. We Christians are called to show love to our friends and enemies alike. We are called to care for the poor, help those in need, work for good and against injustice. Love is the supreme attribute we can show.

Join God's Community, the Church

Fourthly, you need to find some other Christians to hang out with and learn from. Christianity is not about lone-ranger living. We are saved from self-centredness and individualism into God's community, the church. Christianity is not about a private faith – it is about friendships and growing with others. The New Testament describes others in the church as our brothers and sisters.

Remember in our first chapter we discussed how God originally intended that we live with him *and together* in a glorious community of love. Unfortunately due to the rupture, that original community of humanity has been tragically fragmented. When you accept Jesus as your saviour and Lord you become part of the restored community of God's people on earth. This is the church – the gathered people of God.

Churches (that is, individual church organisations) come in all shapes, sizes and forms. No church is perfect – indeed, the church has lost the plot on many occasions and far too often does not reflect God's ideals. But there are also many great churches in a whole range of denominations that seek to honour God. You can tell those that are faithful to God's purposes by their commitment to the truth, their sense of love, openness, acceptance, grace, freedom and positivity.

Where to from here?

Such churches are passionate about talking about Jesus, draw their beliefs from the Bible first and foremost, want to share this message with those who have not yet found Jesus, and are dedicated to love. They believe in the present day work of the Spirit in the lives of believers. They are deeply concerned about others in the wider community. They work to see people won to Christ. They understand the big project of God, encouraging people to work in their professions for God and aiming to see God's project restored in every corner of the world. They care for the poor and marginalised and welcome all people. They are not concerned about money and growing their own empires, they are trying to make the world a better place. Their leaders are not autocratic megalomaniacs who try to control people – rather they are servants who lead out of love.

So how do you go about joining God's church? In one sense you are automatically a part of the church through becoming a believer in Jesus. However, living as a Christian involves participation in a local community of faith with whom we meet regularly for worship, nurture, support, mission and service.[6] Joining a local church starts by going along on Sunday.[7] Find out the service times (phone the church or check their website) and then experience first-hand what the church is like. If you believe this is the right church for you, start attending every week. As you are welcomed, introduce yourself to the people and the leaders. This is your new family. Each church has its own way of including new people. Sometimes people stand back and don't get involved. I encourage you not to be one of those spectators, but become a full member and participate in church life.

Entry into the church also involves baptism. To be baptised means to be 'immersed under water.[8] Jesus was baptised, and from the beginning of Christian history, this practice has been the way new believers have joined God's church. It may seem a little unusual, but to be baptised is a powerful experience. Going under the water is symbolic of dying – being buried and rising with Christ. The water symbolises your sins being washed away. Ask the leaders of your church what is involved and follow through. Usually the baptism service involves standing in water (often in a specially-built baptismal pool or in some other water that is deep enough). The pastor (or another leader) will then baptise you in the name of the Father, Son and Holy Spirit by gently immersing you in the water for a few moments. Seeing you get baptised will inspire others to follow Jesus more passionately.[9]

Another thing that happens in church is what is called Communion, the Eucharist, or the 'Lord's Supper'. The people eat bread and drink wine to remember the death of Jesus. The bread symbolises Jesus' body broken for us, while the wine (or grape juice) recalls Jesus' blood shed for us. Some churches have communion services every week, others less often. When it occurs, it is a solemn and special time to remember Jesus dying for us and the world. As we take communion, we join with the other members of the church to remember Jesus' death, to thank him, ask his forgiveness, and resolve to live for him with everything we have.[10]

I recommend you look around for a church that has such a focus and get involved. Ask God to lead you to just the right church for you, and he will.

Live It Out in Every Part of Your Life

Some people think Christianity is merely a personal private affair of the heart, a spiritual matter. They have a sort of 'go to church on a Sunday and do what you want to do for the rest of the week' approach. This is not what God is about. He wants to be a part of every aspect of our lives. We are to be his people 24/7, not just one hour a week on a Sunday. He is interested in our families, our workplaces and the work we do, our sports clubs and our friendships. In other words, he is interested in every aspect of your existence.

He loves your family and wants to be involved in it, helping you and your loved ones become all that he wants them to be. He is deeply concerned about your marriage or your singleness, your children, brothers, sisters and parents. He welcomes you to him no matter what relational issues you have had in the past.

If you run a business he wants to be a part of it, blessing it and helping you run it in a way that honours him and reflects his Kingdom lifestyle. If you are an artist, remember that God is an artist too and wants you to express your creativity. If your love is science, God is the ultimate scientific genius who wants you to explore his creation and discover those things that can benefit humanity. If you are a sportsperson God is interested in your sport. He wants you to succeed, he will help you in your training and he wants you to bring his principles into your sporting life. Remember that success is not always winning the race, it is winning in life.

He wants you to work together with him as a transformer of his world. He wants his people to cast influence in every area of life. There is no part of human existence that he is not interested in, because it is all his world. In all of your life seek to see God at work, seek to please God, ask him to be involved in leading and guiding you and, above all, show those around you his love.

Read and Learn

Christianity is not only about believing, important though this is. It is about adding knowledge to our faith,[11] deepening our understanding and constantly modifying and expanding our understanding of God, life, ourselves, relationships, the world and others. We are designed to ponder big questions like: Who is God? What does it mean to be human? What is God's plan for the world? What does it mean to be a Christian in a fallen world?

Jesus called his followers 'disciples'. When we hear that word we immediately think of 'discipline', and that is important, but in Bible times it meant a 'learner' or a 'student' – someone dedicated to learning the ways of their master and living out the master's teachings. So I encourage you to be a learner. At the end of this booklet is an appendix that lists books and websites you can read and consider to help deepen your understanding.[12]

Don't make the mistake that many zealous Christians have made over the years. Sometimes people throw away their interest in 'worldly things' – they stop listening to 'secular' music etc and only read the Bible and other 'spiritual' books. God wants us to be interested in the world and what makes it tick. Clearly, there are some things that we should not devote our time to – things that are evil, corrupt or which lead us into sin. However, God wants us to be informed and to relate to the people in the world around us. We should be interested in the news, history, culture, politics, economics, medicine, health, literature, music and all that makes us human. In fact, I would suggest we Christians should be the best read, most knowledgeable people on earth for 'the earth is the Lord's and everything in it'.[13] So be a student of God, the Bible (which is foundational) and all that makes us human.

Pass the Message On

The last thing Jesus said to his disciples before his ascension was to pass on his message to the world. If you have accepted the message in this book, you are now commissioned to spread it. Christians should never refuse to share the message about Jesus – we are holding onto information that brings eternal life!

Jesus wants us to tell everyone. He wants us to pass it on to our families, our workmates and social and sporting friends – that is, the people we are already in contact with. Although you may not realise it, he has governed your existence and strategically placed you in the environment you live in. He wants you to live out your faith there so that the people around you can hear this message and experience a saving relationship with God.

He does not want you to do this in an artificial way or through 'Bible-bashing'. He wants you to do it naturally. Most importantly he wants us to live out our faith with love, showing God's grace through our actions and attitudes of mercy and grace.

There are many ways to share the message, whether it is through a book, with a natural conversation over a coffee or a meal, on holiday, or in the car as you travel. The message spreads best through existing relationships, through the message being given with gentleness, respect and love.

One way you can do this, if you have found it helpful, is to give them this book. Another way is to tell your friends and family how Jesus has changed your life (Christians calls this your 'testimony'). If it is true that God wants everyone to live with him forever in a glorious and exciting relationship, then they need to hear about it. It is up to us to tell them.

But we should never be obnoxious when we share the message. The most important thing is that we show others the message through our attitudes and actions – helping them, loving them and caring for them. Christianity is not about telling people a message without showing the message with our whole lives. When we meet people with different views, we show them respect, we listen to them – we do not bombard them with arrogance and judgementalism. Rather, we gently and graciously talk about the love of God. When we offer them the story, it is 'no-strings-attached', and it is really up to them what they want to do with it. We pray for them and want them to say yes because, if they do, they will become a friend of God, and live with him forever. This is God's dream. Remember, God and the heavenly community of angels have a party to celebrate every time a person says yes to Jesus.[14]

Be a Cosmic Transformer!

Always keep God's big plan in mind. We are appointed by God to work with him to be transformers, working with him by his Spirit, to change the world. This is God's 'cosmission' – his mission to the cosmos. To reiterate once more, God wants this world to be restored in every dimension to his glory and intention. This means he needs his people in every part of the community. That's good news because becoming a Christian doesn't mean we stop being who we are. On the contrary, being a Christian is about being who you really are, and who you were created to be. True Christianity is about being authentic. It means bringing everything we are and do under the lordship of Christ, living our lives in the world for God. We are called to be 'in the world but not of it' – that is, living out our humanity amongst the people around us, but doing so without falling into sin. God loves to take the 'natural' and make it 'supernatural'.

Jesus did not turn his back on the world – he hung out with sinners. He was their friend! Unlike the religious leaders of his day, he was not offended by or afraid of those who were seen as 'unclean'.[15] Paul also encouraged Christians to remain in their vocations and lives after they were converted.[16] He urged believers married to unbelievers to remain in their marriages to see their spouses come to faith through love and grace.[17] He anticipated that believers would spend time at the homes of unbelievers and outsiders, and that unbelievers would come to

Christian gatherings.[18] Although he believed he had the right to be paid as a 'minister', he chose to be a working man, interacting in the marketplace with normal people, working in a workshop sewing tents and setting an example to others.[19] He encouraged believers to follow this pattern, providing for themselves and working to the best of their abilities.[20] As we go about our daily work and lives, God's project is achieved and people are won to Christ by hearing the good news about Jesus and through practical love and mercy.

Conclusion

All in all, God is ultimately looking for our allegiance to him. He hopes that we will realise that he exists. He wants us to see the signs of his existence in creation and the flow of history. He has created us and invites us to live with him for eternity. He wants us to see that he has been to earth as a man, revealing who God is, showing us what God is like. Jesus showed us that God is real – that he is a gentle, loving creator who cares for us deeply. He is a God who heals, comforts, transforms and restores.

He is not a God who will use his power to coerce us into allegiance. Instead he aims to win us over through serving us, sacrificing himself for us, even going through the most horrendous unjust suffering and death for us. He wants us to recognise that the resurrection of Jesus is the crucial moment in history. It declares that he is the one we should follow. He wants us to believe. He wants us to turn from sin and follow him. He wants us to say yes to him. He wants us to join his team and work with him for the transformation of every part of his world. He wants to pour his Spirit into our lives, restore us and empower us, and send us out into his world to be cosmic transformers. He wants to restore creation, form a new humanity, and see his world become what it can be. You are called to this. Will you accept his glorious offer?

Questions For Reflection

1. Considering who God is and what he has done, what words do you think best capture what it means to respond to God appropriately? Think of words like believe, repent, follow, worship etc.
2. What does it mean to be saved by God's grace and not works, yet then work for him? How are the two notions related?
3. What does God want from those who have accepted his salvation?
4. Having read my story, write down your story and go and share it with others.
5. How can you live your life as a cosmic transformer in your part of the world? What would that mean?
6. Have you given your life to Jesus? What is stopping you?
7. Are you living fully for Jesus? What is stopping you?

And Finally…

Thank you for taking the time to read this explanation of the message that has changed my life and that continues to change the world. I pray that you will be blessed in every way by God. I encourage you to live for God with all that you are and have. If you are still not sure about all this, speak out to God and ask him to lead you to a place of certainty. And if you have decided to follow Jesus may God bless you more richly than you could ever think or imagine!

If you wish to contact the author, Mark Keown, with questions, comments or thoughts, he is a lecturer in the New Testament at Laidlaw College in Auckland, New Zealand, and can be reached at mkeown@laidlaw.ac.nz.

APPENDIX ONE
AM I REALLY A SINNER?

This section is designed to test whether or not you are really a sinner, using the standards listed in the Bible as a benchmark. First, let's have a look at the Ten Commandments and the two Greatest Commandments to check out whether you and I really are flawed in this way.

The Ten Commandments were given by God to Moses on Mt Sinai. They represent the heart of God's relationship with Israel. They were the terms of the covenant (or 'agreement') given by God for the good of Israel so that they would experience life as it should be. If the people of God adhered to these commandments, God who had saved them out of slavery in Egypt would be their king, caring for them and protecting them.

At no point did Jesus overthrow the Ten Commandments; rather, he endorsed them and reinterpreted them (see Mark 10:29-31). The Two Great Commandments are Jesus' summary of the Ten Commandments, designed for his people and for all humanity. As you read them, ask yourself whether you have lived by God's essential principles:

The Ten Commandments:

LAW 1: 'You shall have no other gods before me.'

The first four commandments relate to our human relationship with God. This first law means: is there anything you have made more important than God in your life? It could be a person (e.g. a wife/husband), a group (e.g. a family, a group of friends), an activity (e.g. work, sport, hobby), yourself (e.g. your body, image), an object (e.g. money, a car) etc. In other words, has God been the number one thing in your life? Have you kept this principle for your whole life without exception? If you are honest with yourself, your answer will be no! If this is the case, according to this law you are a sinner.

LAW 2: 'You shall not make for yourself an idol in the form of anything in heaven above or on the earth beneath or in the waters below. You shall not bow down to them or worship them.'

This is similar to the first commandment but related to the culture of the world Israel was established in. It applies to the practice of worshiping graven images found in the Ancient Near Eastern world of Jesus' time and in many nations today. Essentially for us it raises a similar question to the first; do we put any idea (e.g. a philosophy like communism), activity, belief, person, graven image etc before God? Again, the answer to the question, have we kept this law?, must be no. Before my conversion, my idol was sport, myself, and a desire to achieve my own selfish ambitions. I have failed to live up to God's standard in this. Have you? If we are honest with ourselves, we all know that we have failed in this area. So, by the standard of this law, you are a sinner.

LAW 3: 'You shall not misuse the name of the LORD your God, for the LORD will not hold anyone guiltless who misuses his name.'

This can mean simply using God's name as a swear word (e.g. 'Christ!' or 'Oh my God!'). But it also has a greater implication. It means abusing God by not honouring him for the great things he has done. It is evident when we curse God for bad things that happen, but fail to thank him for the good things that occur. It is seen when we remember him when times are tough and ask for his help or healing, but the rest of the time we ignore him or forget he's there. Basically we are using him. It may mean blaming him for the bad things that happen when in actual fact it is our own actions or the actions of other people (e.g. a drunk driver) that have caused the damage. Most, if not all of us, at one time or another have done these things. So again the answer to the question, have we kept this law?, is no! On the basis of this law, you are a sinner.

LAW 4: 'Remember the Sabbath day by keeping it holy. Six days you shall labour and do all your work, but the seventh day is a Sabbath to the Lord your God. On it you shall not do any work, neither you, nor your son or daughter, nor your manservant or maidservant, nor your animals, nor the alien within your gates.'

This means that we should remember to keep one day of the week for the purpose of rest, worship and recreation. In the Old Testament the 'Sabbath' was Friday evening and Saturday. The Jews had a lot of other laws to ensure this was kept, and the practice became legalistic. Jesus redefined this law making it clear that the real principles behind it were to ensure we took a day off each week for rest, recreation and worship of God for our own good. We could still do 'work' on the Sabbath that benefited others (e.g. medical assistance) but on the whole, we should rest, recreate, and worship together. I'm sure that, like me, you have not kept this principle through your whole life. So the answer to the question, have we kept this law?, is no! On the basis of this law, you are a sinner.

LAW 5: 'Honour your father and your mother, so that you may live long in the land the Lord your God is giving you.'

This is the first of the 'interpersonal relational' laws. We are commanded to obey, respect and honour our parents. The only point at which the Bible approves of anything other is when there is a conflict between obeying God and our parents. In those instances, we obey God first, but we do so with humility, gentleness and love. Note the reason given for keeping this law: 'so that you may live long…' This is repeated in the New Testament and should be understood spiritually. That is, if we honour our parents, society will be peaceful, the law and worship of God will be retained from generation to generation, and we will know the peace and relationship God has for us. Hence, it is a law that is for our good as individuals and more importantly, families and communities. It is clear as we look at the world that this law is continually abused. It is almost more common *not* to obey our parents – teenage rebellion (for example) is par for the course in the western world. The western mindset also tends to view the elderly as a 'burden' in a society that idolises youthfulness. Can any of us then say that we have kept this law? I certainly cannot! I am certain that if we are all honest, there have been times when we have not honoured our parents; so the answer to the question, have we kept this law?, is no! So, on the basis of this law, you are a sinner.

LAW 6: 'You shall not murder.'

At face value, this commandment means that we must not take the life of another in anger or unjustly. Most Christians would apply this to the unborn infant (abortion), the taking of another life in anger or unjustly (homicide) and assisted suicide (euthanasia). However, Jesus took it further and suggested that to harbour murderous thoughts was essentially the same as murdering the other person (Matthew 5:21-22). In other words, murder begins in the heart. Hence, while we may not be guilty of murder to the degree that we have physically taken another person's life, we are all guilty of the desire to destroy others especially when they have harmed us or other innocent people – the desire for revenge falls into this category. So the answer to the question, have we kept this law?, is no! So, according to the standards of God, you are a sinner.

LAW 7: 'You shall not commit adultery.'

Here 'commit adultery' is a summary term for 'sexual immorality'. The Bible emphatically rejects all sexual relationships outside of a heterosexual, life-long, committed, faithful and loving marriage. This seems radical in our modern society but Jesus was even more radical in his interpretation of this verse, suggesting that even to lust after another person is to commit adultery (Matthew 5:27-30). This is because each person is a precious creation in God's sight and deserves to be honoured, loved and respected as a person and not as an object of desire. It is also because marriage and families are the basis of an ordered society. While individual sexually immoral acts and relationships may appear harmless, in fact they cut to the core of an ordered society and God's intention for his world. When we think of this law in its fullest sense we are all at least guilty of sexually desiring another person and, in many cases, of engaging in adulterous relationships. So the answer to the question, have we kept this law?, is no! In God's eyes, by this law, you are a sinner.

LAW 8: 'You shall not steal.'

This commandment is a general statement against taking another person's property. This applies to a paper clip at work, a person's copyrighted idea in a book, a pirated or downloaded illegal CD or DVD, or taking another person's integrity, etc. Without question none of us have lived flawlessly in this area. So the answer to the question, have we kept this law?, is no! Again, you are a sinner by God's standards.

LAW 9: 'You shall not give false testimony against your neighbour.'

This commandment can be applied to a legal context where a witness gives false evidence against someone to see them convicted. But in its broadest sense it applies to all forms of lying, false representation or of failing to keep our word. As in the case of stealing, we have all spoken falsely on numerous occasions, ranging from 'white-lies' to major tax fraud. So the answer to the question, have we kept this law?, is no! So, you are a sinner by the standards of God.

LAW 10: 'You shall not covet your neighbour's house. You shall not covet your neighbour's wife, or his manservant or maidservant, his ox or donkey, or anything that belongs to your neighbour.'

This commandment is seen as a summary law covering the desire to possess other things, other people, or the desire to gain a reputation and wealth etc. It is an endemic trait in all humanity that we look at what others are and have and want to be like them or have what they have. Greed, 'keeping up with the Joneses' and consumerism fall into this category. Without doubt, all of us are guilty of this. So the answer to the question, have we kept this law?, is no! This summary law cuts to our motives; we are all guilty before God, hence, we are sinners.

The Two Greatest Commandments

Jesus specifically stated that these laws were not superseded by his teaching. Rather, he explained the original intent and purpose behind the Ten Commandments. He rejected some of the Old Testament Jewish applications of the laws and instead gave precedence to the spirit of the law. He summarised them into two statements, also found in the Old Testament,[1] and said that 'there is no commandment greater than these'. These two laws (found in Mark 12:29-31) form the basis of Christian ethics.

The Greatest Commandment: 'The most important one is this… Love the Lord your God with all your heart and with all your soul and with all your mind and with all your strength.'

This is a summary of the first four of the Ten Commandments and drives to the heart of what it means to have a relationship with God. It involves four 'alls', indicating that loving God with our whole beings and total strength is the number one priority – that is, 'love the Lord your God with *everything you've got!*' This includes our time, our gifts, our wealth, and our dreams and ambitions. These things are to be put at God's disposal. When we measure our lives against this standard, without exception, we all fall short. Any thought, act or word that did not love God means we have failed him. So the answer to the question, have we kept this law?, is clearly no! Hence, we are all sinners before God.

The Second Greatest Commandment: The second is this: "Love your neighbour as yourself. There is no commandment greater than these.'

This is a summary of the last six of the Ten Commandments and means that every thought, act or deed towards other people should be governed by our love for them. Any thought, act or deed that does not come out of love and does not benefit others is a violation of the law. When Jesus was quizzed on what he meant by 'your neighbour' he told a story that clearly indicated all humanity, especially those in need, are our neighbours – this includes our enemies and even those who cause us harm. Again I suggest, without exception, we have failed in this. We are guilty of injustice, oppression, putting others down and more. So the answer to the question, have we kept this law?, is no! Hence we are all sinners by the standards of God.

It is clear then that we are all sinners on multiple counts. As such, we, like all instances of evil, will face God when it comes time for him to remove evil from his universe. Our only way out is through the path blazed for us by the Saviour and Lord of the world, Jesus (see chapter three).

APPENDIX TWO
OTHER RESOURCES

This is a list of books that I and other Christians have recommended. It purposely contains a range of Christian perspectives to challenge you and to show that Christianity is wonderfully diverse. Enjoy!

Becoming a Christian and Christian Faith

Affirm Booklets	A range of books on Christian life; see http://www.presaffirm.org.nz/resources.htm.
Badke, William.	*The Hitchhikers Guide to the Meaning of Everything*. Kregel Publications, 2005.
Bell, Rob.	*Velvet Elvis: Repainting the Christian Faith*. Zondervan, 2005.
Dickson, John.	*Simple Christianity*. Matthias Media, 1999.
Elredge, John.	*The Story God is Telling and the Role That is Yours to Play*. Thomas Nelson, 2004.
Green, Michael.	*What is Christianity?* Lion, 1981.
Gumbel, N.	*Questions of Life. A Practical Introduction to the Christian Faith*. Kingsway, 1993.
Guiness, Os.	*Long Journey Home: A Guide to Your Search for the Meaning of Life*. WaterBrook Press, 2001.
Lewis, C.S.	*Mere Christianity*. MacMillan, 1952, 2009.
McGrath, A.	*Christianity: An Introduction*. Blackwell, 2006.
McManus, Erwin R.	*Wide Awake: The Future is Waiting For You*. Thomas Nelson, 2008.
Malins, Ian.	*Come to Me: A Series of 5 Studies Explaining the Way to Meet Jesus Personally and How to Become a Christian*. Christian Books Melanesia Inc., 2001.
Miller, Donald.	*Blue Like Jazz: Nonreligious Thoughts on Christian Spirituality*. Thomas Nelson, 2003.
Piper, John.	*Don't Waste Your Life*. Wheaton: Crossway Books, 2007 (see also www.desiringgod.org/media/pdf/books_dwyl/dwyl_full.pdf).
Stott, John.	*Basic Christianity*. Eerdmans, 2008.
Strobel, Lee.	*The Case For Faith: A Journalist Investigates the Toughest Objections to Christianity*. Zondervan, 2002.

Sweet, Leonard.	*Jesus Drives Me Crazy! Lose Your Mind, Find Your Soul*. Zondervan, 2003.
Video Series:	*The Alpha Course: A Practical Introduction to the Christian Faith*. HTB Publications, 1993; alphacourse.org; info@alphacourse.org
Wright, N.T.	*Simply Christian: Why Christianity Makes Sense*. HarperSanFrancisco, 2006.
Walker, Peter	*The Jesus Way: The Essential Christian Starter Kit*. Monarch Books, 2009.
Yancey, Philip.	*Reaching for the Invisible God: What Can We Expect to Find*. Zondervan, 2000.
Website,	http://www.matthiasmedia.com.au/mmstore/mtmdvd.html?id=DDmFzuFr

God

Collicut, Joanna., McGrath, Alistair.	*The Dawkins Delusion? Atheist Fundamentalism and the Denial of the Divine*. IVP, 2007.
Geisler, Norman L., Turek, Frank., Limbaugh, David.	*I Don't Have Enough Faith to Be an Atheist*. Crossway Books, 2004.
Green, Michael.	*My God*. Eagle, 1992.
Keller, Tim.	*The Reason for God: Belief in an Age of Skepticism*. Dutton, 2008.
Keller, Tim.	*The Prodigal God: Rediscovering the Heart of the Christian Faith*. Dutton, 2008.
Packer, J.I.	*Knowing God*. IVP, 1973.

Jesus

Buckingham, Jamie.	*The Nazarene*. Kingsway, 1991.
Strobel, L.	*Christ: A Journalist's Personal Invitation of the Evidence for Jesus*. Zondervan, 2001.
Strobel, L.	*The Case for the Real Jesus: A Journalist Investigates Current Attacks on The Identity of Christ*. Zondervan, 2007.
Wright, C.	*Knowing Jesus through the Old Testament*. IVP, 1995.
Yancey, Philip.	*The Jesus I Never Knew*. Zondervan, 2005.

What's God Up To…?

Grace

Dickson, John. *Jesus A Short Life*. Lion, 2008.
Yancey, Philip. *What's So Amazing About Grace*. Zondervan, 2003.

History of Christianity

Noll, Mark. *Turning Points: Decisive Moments in the History of Christianity*. Baker Academic, 1997, 2001.
Shelley, Bruce L. *Church History in Plain Language*. 3rd Ed. Thomas Nelson, 2008.
Stark, Rodney. *The Victory of Reason: How Christianity Led to Freedom, Capitalism, and Western Success*. Random House Trade Paperbacks, 2006.

Reading the Bible

Alexander, David.,
Alexander, Pat. *The Lion Handbook to the Bible*. Lion, 1983.
Bartholomew, Craig G.,
Goheen, Michael W. *The Drama of Scripture: Finding Our Place in the Biblical Story*. SPCK Publishing, 2006.
Beynon, Nigel.
Sach, Andrew. *Dig Deeper! Tools to Unearth the Bible's Treasure*. IVP, 2005.
Davis Ellen F.,
Hays, Richard B. *The Art of Reading Scripture*. Eerdmans, 2003.
Gumbel, Nicky. *30 Days: A 30 Days Practical Introduction to Reading the Bible*. Alpha International, 2001.
Lee-Thorp, Karen. *A Compact Guide to the Christian Life*. Colorado: Navpress, 2001.
Fee G.D.,
Stuart, D. *How to Read the Bible for All It's Worth*. Zondervan, 1993
Fee G.D.,
Stuart, D. *How to Read the Bible Book By Book*. Zondervan, 2002.
McKnight, Scot. *Blue Parakeet: Rethinking How You Read the Bible*. Zondervan, 2008.
Mears, Henrietta C. *What the Bible is All About*. Gospel Light Publications, 1998.
Pilavachi, Mike.,
Croft, Andy. *Storylines: Your Map to Understanding the Bible*. David C. Cook, 2010.
Roberts, Vaughan. *God's Big Picture: Tracing the Story-Line of the Bible*. IVP, 2003.
Stibbes, Alan M. *Search the Scriptures: A Study Guide to the Bible*. IVP, 1949/67. (Read through the Bible over 3 years with questions).

Strom, M.	*The Symphony of Scripture: Making Sense of the Bible's Many Themes.* P & R. Publishing, 2001.
Ward, Tim.	*Words of Life.* IVP Academic, 2009.
Wright, N.T.	*For Everyone Series* (Paul, John, Matthew, Luke etc). A great series of commentaries to read along with the Bible text to increase understanding.
Yancey, Philip.	*The Bible Jesus Read.* Zondervan, 1999.

Christian Testimony

Cruz, Nicky., Buckingham, Jamie.	*Run Baby Run.* Bridge Logos, 1968.
Furst, Peter.	*The Winning Edge: Sports Stars Share Their Spiritual Journeys.* Lime Grove House Publishing, 2002.
Hattaway, Paul., Liu, Zhenying.	*The Heavenly Man.* Kregel Publications, 2004.
Isaac, Tuhoe., Haami, Bradford.	*True Red.* True Red, 2007 (see also www.frontofthebox.co.nz/Our-Company/Media-Releases/MenuId/20.aspx?PageId=144).
Lewis, C.S.	*Surprised by Joy.* Harcourt, Bruce, 1956.
Pullinger, Jackie., Quicke, Andrew.	*Chasing the Dragon: One Woman's Struggle Against the Darkness of Hong Kong's Drug Dens.* Gospel Light, 2007.
Sheikh, Bilquis., Schneider, Richard H.	*I Dared to Call Him Father: The True Story of a Woman Who Discovers What Happens When She Gives Herself To God Completely.* Christian Art, 2000.
Ten Boom, Corrie., Sherrill, John., Sherrill, Elizabeth,	*The Hiding Place.* G.K. Hall, 1973.
Stott, John.	*Why I Am A Christian: This Is My Story.* IVP, 2003.
Wilkerson, David.	*The Cross and the Switchblade.* Pyramid, 1974.
Anthony, Tony.	*Taming the Tiger: From the Depths of Hell to the Heights of Glory.* STL Ltd, 2004.
Lungu, Stephen., Coomes, Anne.	*Out of the Black Shadows.* Kregel Publications, 2001.
Video Series:	*Journeys*: http://secure.intellihost.co.nz/greatjourneys.co.nz

What's God Up To…?

Questions Answered

Boa, K.,
Moody, L. *I'm Glad You Asked. In-depth Answers to Difficult Questions About Christianity.* Victor Books, 1982.
Bock, Darrell L.,
Zacharias, Ravi. *Can I Trust The Bible?* IVP, 2007.
Geisler, Norman L. *Christian Apologetics.* Baker, 1976.
Geisler, Norman L. *Unshakable Foundations: Contemporary Answers to Crucial Questions About Christian Faith.* Bethany House, 2001.
Gumbel, N. *Searching Issues. Tackling Seven Common Objections to the Christian Faith.* Kingsway, 1994.
Gumbel, N. *Questions of Life.* Gardner Books, 2007.
Orr-Ewing, Amy. *But Is It Real? Answering 10 Common Objections to the Christian Faith.* IVP, 2008.
Orr-Ewing, Amy. *Is the Bible Intolerant? And Sexist? And Oppressive? And Homophobic? And Outdated? And Irrelevant?* IVP, 2006.
Orr-Ewing, Amy. *Why Trust the Bible? Answers to 10 Tough Questions.* IVP, 2008.
McDowell J.,
Stewart, Don. *Answers: Tough Questions Sceptics Ask About the Christian Faith.* Campus Crusade for Christ, 1980.
Zacharias, Ravi.,
Geisler, Norman L. *Who Made God? And Answers to Over 100 Other Tough Questions of Faith.* Zondervan, 2003.
Zacharias, Ravi. *Is Believing God Irrational?* IVP, 2008.
Websites: www.gotquestions.org or www.rzim.org/AP/home.aspx or www.equip.org or www.impactapologetics.com

Creation

Geisler, Norman L. *Knowing the Truth About Creation: How it Happened and What it Means For Us.* Servant Publications, 1989.
Nelson Paul.,
Newman R.C.,
Van Till, Howard J. *Three Views on Creation and Evolution.* Zondervan, 1999.
Peters, Ted.,
Hewlett, Martinez. *Can You Believe in God And Evolution? A Guide for the Perplexed.* Abingdon, 2001.
Strobel, Lee. *The Case for a Creator: A Journalist Investigates Scientific Evidence That Points Toward God.* Zondervan, 2004.

Appendices

Video:	Focus on the Family, *Unlocking the Mystery of Life. The case for Intelligent Design*. www.family.org.nz; mail@focus.org.nz

The Resurrection

Geisler, Norman L.	*The Battle for the Resurrection*. Thomas Nelson, 1989.
Green, Michael.	*The Empty Cross of Jesus*. Hodder and Stoughton, 1984.
Morison, Frank.	*Who Moved the Stone*. STL Books, 1930.
Strobel, Lee.	*The Case for Easter: A Journalist Investigates the Evidence for the Resurrection*. Zondervan, 2003.

Heaven and Hell

Crockett, V.	*Four Views on Hell*. Zondervan, 1992.
Milne, Bruce.	*The Message of Heaven and Hell: Grace and Destiny*. IVP, 2003.

Predestination and Freewill

Feinberg, S.	
Basinger, D.	
Basinger, R.	*Predestination & Free Will: Four Views of Divine Sovereignty & Human Freedom*. IVP, 1986.

Suffering and Evil

Carson, D.	*How Long O Lord? Reflections on Suffering and Evil*. Baker Book House, 1990.
Wright, Chris.	*The God I Don't Understand*. Zondervan, 2009.
Yancey, Philip.	*Where is God When it Hurts?* Zondervan, 2007.

General Christian Living

Andews, Dave.	*Christi-anarchy: Discovering a Radical Spirituality of Compassion*. Lion, 1999.
Arterbum, Stephen.	*Being Christian: Exploring Where You Are, God and Life Connect*. Bethany House, 2009.
Bell, Rob,	NOOMA (see nooma.com).
Bell, Rob.,	

What's God Up To...?

Golden, Don.	*Jesus Wants to Save Christians: A Manifesto for the Church in Exile.* Zondervan, 2008.
Benner, David G.	*Surrender to Love: Discovering the Heart of Christian Spirituality.* IVP, 2003.
Bonhoeffer, D.	*The Cost of Discipleship.* SCM Canterbury Press, 2001.
Bridges, Jerry.	*The Practice of Godliness.* Navpress, 1983.
Carson, Don.	*Basics For Believers: An Exposition of Philippians.* Baker Books, 1996.
Claiborne, Shane.	*The Irresistible Revolution: Living As An Ordinary Radical.* Zondervan, 2006.
Colson Charles W., Pearcey, Nancy.	*How Now Shall We Live?* Tyndale House Publishers, 1999.
Foster, Richard.	*Celebration of Discipline: The Path To Spiritual Growth.* HarperSanFrancisco, 1988.
Galli, Mark.	*Jesus Mean and Wild: The Unexpected Love of an Untamable God.* Baker Books, 2008.
Green, M.	*After Alpha.* Kingsway, 1998.
Gumbel, Nicky.	*A Life Worth Living.* Kingsway, 1994.
Gumbel, Nicky.	*Questions of Life: A Practical Introduction to the Christian Faith.* David C. Cook Publishing Company, 2002.
Keller, Tim.	*Counterfeit Gods: The Empty Promises of Money, Sex, and Power, and the Only Hope that Matters.* Dutton, 2009.
McManus, Erwin R.	*The Barbarian Way: Unleash the Untamed Faith Within.* Thomas Nelson, 2005.
Malins, Ian.	*Come Follow Me: Studies in Discipleship.* Christian Books Melanesia, 1985.
Manning, Brendon.	*The Rugamuffin Gospel: Embracing the Unconditional love of God.* Authentic, 2006.
Manning, Brendon.	*Abba's Child: The Cry of the Heart for Intimate Belonging.* NavPress, 1994.
Rufus, Rob.	*Living the Grace of God.* Authentic Media, 2007.
Sayers, Mark.	*The Trouble With Paris: Following Jesus in a World of Plastic Promises.* Thomas Nelson, 2008.
Stott, J.R.W.	*The Contemporary Christian: Applying God's Word to Today's World.* IVP, 1992.
Stott, J.R.W.	*New Issues Facing Christians Today.* Marshall Pickering, 1999.
Watson, David.	*Discipleship.* Hodder & Stoughton, 2001.
Warren, Rick.	*The Purpose Driven Life: What On Earth Am I Here For?* Zondervan, 2002.
Wright, N.T.	*Following Jesus: Biblical Reflections on Discipleship.* Eerdmans, 1995.

Wright, N.T.	www.ntwrightpage.com (a whole lot of stuff here, articles, lectures).
Zacharias, Ravi.	*Beyond Opinion: Living the Faith We Defend.* Thomas Nelson, 2008.

The Cross

McKnight, S.	*A Community Called Atonement.* Abingdon, 2007.
Strobel, L.	
Poole, G.	*Experiencing the Passion of Jesus.* Zondervan, 2004.
Stott, J.R.W.	*The Cross of Christ.* IVP, 1986.

Sharing the Faith

Geisler, Norman L.	*Living Loud: Defending Your Faith.* Broadman and Holman, 2002.
Green, Michael.	*Evangelism – Now and Then.* IVP, 1979.
Harley, Rob.	*The Power of the Story: Touching the Lives of Listeners.* End Results, 2001.
Hybels, Bill.	
Mittenberg, Mark.	*Becoming a Contagious Christian.* Zondervan, 1994.
Watson, David.	*I Believe in Evangelism.* Hodder & Stoughton, 1976.

Christian Theology

Erickson, M.	*Christian Theology.* Baker, 1983-85.
Geisler, N.	*Systematic Theology.* Bethany House, 2002.
Higton, M.	*Christian Doctrine.* SCM-Canterbury Press Ltd, 2008.
Jinkins & M.	
Torrance, Alan.	*Invitation to Theology.* IVP, 2001.
Milne, B.	*Know the Truth. A Handbook of Christian Belief.* IVP, 1998.
Olsen, R.	*The Mosaic of Christian Belief: Twenty Centuries of Unity and Diversity.* IVP/Apollos, 2002.

Women in Ministry

Belleville, Linda L.	
Blomberg, Craig L.	
Keener, Craig S.	
Schreiner, Thomas R.	*Two Views of Women in Ministry.* Zondervan, 2005.

What's God Up To…?

Christians in Society

Bell, Rob.	*Everything is Spiritual*. Zondervan, 2007.
Boyd, Gregory A.	*The Myth of a Christian Nation: How the Quest for Political Power is Destroying the Church*. Zondervan, 2007.
Buxton, Graham.	*Celebrating Life: Beyond the Sacred-Secular Divide*. STL Distribution North America, 2007.
Cameron, Julia.	*The Artist's Way: A Spiritual Path to Higher Creativity*. J.P. Tarcher/Putnam, 2002.
Campolo, Tony.	*Red Letter Christians: A Citizen's Guide to Faith and Politics*. Gospel Light, 2008.
Dunham, Annette.	*Soul Purpose: Making a Difference in Life and Work*. NavPress (NZ), 2004.
Gaebelein, Frank. Mackenzie, Alistair.	*The Christian, the Arts and Truth*. Multnomah Press, 1983.
Kirkland, Wayne.	*Integrating Faith and Work Every Day of the Week*. NavPress, 2003.
Platinga, C.	*God's World: A Christian Vision of Faith*. Eerdmans, 2002.
Rookmaaker, H.R.	*Art Needs No Justification*. IVP, 1978.
Turner, Steve. Walsh, Brian.	*A Vision for Christians in the Arts*. IVP, 2001.
Middleton, J. Richard.	*The Transforming Vision: Shaping a Christian World View*. IVP, 1984.
Websites	www.christianityexplored.org; www.seaninternational.com; www.alpha.org.nz

Christmas

Strobel, L.	*The Case for Christmas: A Journalist Investigates the Identity of the Child in the Manger*. Zondervan, 2005.

Novels

Colsen, Jake., Jacobsen, Wayne.	
Coleman, Dave.	*So You Don't Want to Go to Church Anymore*. Windblown Media, 2008.
Lewis, C.S.	*The Chronicles of Narnia*. HarperCollins, 2000 (especially *The Magician's Nephew* [Creation], *The Lion, the Witch and the Wardrobe* [Christ] and *The Last Battle* [The End and Judgement] which all help with understanding theology through allegory.

Lewis, C.S.	*The Great Divorce*. Luther, 2001.
Lewis, C.S.	*The Screwtape Letters*. Whitaker House, 1984.
Young, William P.	*The Shack*. Windblown Media, 2007.

Science and Faith

McGrath, Alister E.	
Lucas, Ernest.,	*Science and Religion: A New Introduction*. Blackwell Publishing, 2010.
Pfundner, Michael	*Think God, Think Science: Conversations on Life, the Universe and Faith*. Authentic Media, 2009.

Sexuality

Bell, Rob.	*Sex God: Exploring the Endless Connections Between Sexuality and Spirituality*. Zondervan, 2008.

NOTES

Chapter 1: Relationship

1. While God is not male or female, I will use the masculine personal pronoun because it emphasises the 'personal' aspect of God. 'It' is too abstract to describe a personal God. 'He/she' is cumbersome.' Hence, I will retain the traditional use of the masculine. Human maleness and femaleness both reflect aspects of God's nature.
2. For further reflection on the arguments for the existence of God see http://plato.stanford.edu/entries/teleological-arguments/; http://plato.stanford.edu/entries/cosmological-argument/; http://plato.stanford.edu/entries/moral-arguments-god/. See also http://plato.stanford.edu/entries/ontological-arguments/ (all sighted Oct, 2009).
3. We call this the cosmological argument for God. It suggests that creation itself points to a cause, a creator. Philosophers have exposed that this is not a *proof* and I agree. However, this universe requires an explanation and God is a strong possibility.
4. This is the teleological argument, the argument from order. Again this is not completely conclusive. However, the beauty, order and complexity of the universe and world can be explained by a God or gods.
5. This is the moral argument for the existence of God. It argues that, while there are differences, there is a common sense of right and wrong in humanity. It can be argued that this is from God.
6. Genesis 1:1 (Note, when reading these references such as this, 1:1 stands for Chapter One Verse One. In the next reference, Job 42:2 stands for Chapter Forty Two, Verse Two. These chapter and verses can be found in the Bible).
7. God is a lot of other things as well, like just, righteous, unchanging and so on. I am highlighting these attributes for this presentation.
8. Job 42:2.
9. Genesis 1:1: 'In the beginning God created the heavens and the earth.'
10. Take for example molecular biology with the complexity of the human cell. Many scientists who have been avowed atheists are realising that the complexity of the human cell defies explanation without resorting to outside intervention from God (see the Focus on the Family 'Intelligent Design' videos in the appendix).
11. 1 John 4:8.
12. Genesis 21:33.
13. 1 Timothy 1:17.
14. See John 3:16; Hebrews 5:9.

Notes

15 Or 'holy' which carries not only the notion of purity but of separateness i.e. God is beyond his creation.
16 Habakkuk 1:13.
17 Psalms 5:4.
18 Christians debate the nature of heaven. Some believe it is another dimension in which God and his realm exists and to which we go at the point of death. Others, like me, argue it will be an earth restored after some divine act of purification (dissolution) in which we will live in a world totally restored, in perfect relationship with God. That is, God's world (heaven) will merge with a renewed purified earth at the climax of all things and heaven and earth will be one.
19 See Genesis 1-2.
20 My own perspective is currently a preference for old age creationism. However, I can see strengths and weaknesses in all positions. I affirm the central truth, 'In the beginning, God created the heavens and the earth.' My faith does not rest on any theory of creation but on faith in Jesus as saviour and Lord (see the remainder of the book).
21 Genesis 1:27.
22 The concept of the image of God also includes other concepts such as being creative as God is. This is good news for scientists, artists, musicians and other creative people; expressing our creativity is part of what we are created for. So whatever your area of creativity, go for it!
23 See Genesis 3:8-9 where God came to walk in the garden with Adam and Eve and was disappointed when he could not find them for they were hiding in guilt, shame and fear.
24 Universal Pictures, 2003.
25 Christians differ on the way these passages should be interpreted. Some consider them symbolic rather than literal. Some consider them literal. Some like me consider them a blend of the literal and symbolic, a real situation with great symbolic meaning. However they are taken, in the biblical story they give the theological basis for understanding existence and the basis upon which life is formed.
26 See Genesis 2:9: 'In the middle of the garden was the tree of life' and 2:16: 'you are free to eat from any tree in the garden; but you must not eat from the tree of the knowledge of good and evil.'
27 This is the doctrine of the Trinity whereby God is one, but is simultaneously and eternally expressed in three manifestations: the Father, the Son and the Spirit. Examples in which the Trinity is seen are Mark 1:10-11 (*Jesus* is baptised, *the Father* speaks, *the Spirit* falls); Matthew 28:20 (baptised in the name of the *Father, Son* and *Spirit*); 1 Corinthians 12:4-6 (spiritual gifts are implanted by the three interchangeably); 2 Corinthians 13:13 (the blessing).

28 This is the idea of God as community, the social trinity. It is also called perichoresis, the community of the Godhead. God is one in community and we who believe in him are drawn into this community.
29 For some idea of what these beings may be like read Ezekiel 1:1-28 and the whole book of Revelation. Note that some Christians do not take this literally.
30 See Philippians 3:20: 'our citizenship is in heaven.'
31 The Aramaic *Abba* which is more intimate than 'Father' and while not quite 'daddy,' is an intimate familial term (Mark 14:36; Romans 8:15).
32 Christians debate whether 'Father' is still an appropriate term for God in light of imperfect human fathers, and that God is not gendered along with patriarchy and so some prefer 'parent,' 'mother,' 'Mother/Father' or simply 'God.' I acknowledge the limitations, but because Jesus used this as his primary mode of address to God, I will retain it.
33 So the first question in the foundational Presbyterian document *The Westminster Shorter Catechism*: Q. 1. What is the chief end of humanity? A. The chief end of man (inclusive of male and female) is to glorify God, and to enjoy him forever. See also John 4:24: 'worshipers who worship God in Spirit and in truth;' Romans 12:1-2: that we offer our 'lives (bodies) as living sacrifices to God.'
34 See Mark 12:29-30 cf. Deuteronomy 6:5. See also the first 4 laws of the 10 Commandments (Exodus 20:3-11).
35 See Luke 15:11: 'there was a Father who had two sons...'
36 See Genesis 2:18: 'The LORD God said, "It is not good for the man to be alone. I will make a helper suitable for him"' and Genesis 2:21-24.
37 See Mark 12:31 cf. Leviticus 19:18. See also the final 6 laws of the 10 Commandments (Ex 20:12-20).
38 One helpful way of thinking about this is the Cross itself. The vertical arm represents the relationship between God and humanity. The horizontal arm represents interpersonal relationships. Both arms are essential to the cross.
39 See for example 1 John 3:16-17: failure to help people in need is a failure to love God.
40 See Genesis 1:28-30.
41 See Genesis 2:25.
42 Most Christians take this literally as a real garden. Others see this as symbolic of the environment where God placed the first humans. Some, like me, see it as a literal garden, but symbolic of the perfection of the first environment.
43 See Genesis 2:9, 16: 'You are *free* to eat from any tree in the garden.' Ironically God revealed the existence of freedom by removing freedom.
44 See Genesis 2:17a: 'but you must not eat from the tree of the knowledge of good and evil.'
45 See Genesis 2:17b: 'for when you eat of it you will surely die.'

Notes

46 Genesis 3:1.
47 Sections that possibly refer to this fall include Isaiah 14: 12-17; Ezekiel 28:12-17; Luke 10:18-20; Revelation 12:7-10 cf. Genesis 6:1-4.
48 Paramount Pictures, 1998.
49 Genesis 3:2: "'You will not surely die," the serpent said to the woman. "For God knows that when you eat of it your eyes will be opened, and you will be like God, knowing good and evil'."
50 We have to be careful here not to imagine that creation put God in any risk in a technical or ontological sense. He is unaffected in his being in any way whatever happens. The risk here is relational; some could choose to reject God and so there is a risk of rejection.
51 Interestingly Jesus taught that more would say 'no' than 'yes'; more would walk the easy wide road to destruction than the narrow hard way to salvation (see Matthew 7:13-14; Luke 13:22-25); yet he was still prepared to create!

Chapter 2: Rupture

1 Traditionally called 'the Fall of Humanity (or Man);' a full account can be read in Genesis 3.
2 Some believe that this was not Satan but merely an animal i.e. a mythological phenomenological account. However, the way in which the biblical writers understand Satan as a snake or serpent, it is better to see this creature as Satan in guise or perhaps the snake as an animal symbolic of God's adversary, Satan. See Luke 10:19; 2 Corinthians 11:3; Revelation 12:9, 14, 15; 20:2.
3 Genesis 2:17; 3:1-2.
4 Genesis 3:4-5.
5 Genesis 2:17. When God said this, he did not mean that they would drop dead. Rather, corruption and death would enter human experience.
6 Some people believe Eve is primarily responsible for the sin, noting what Paul says in 1 Timothy 2:14. However, the text of Genesis makes it clear that Adam was with her at the time, hence Paul's words should not be pushed to this extent. The problem in 1 Timothy 2 is probably women who were uneducated and more liable to deception as a result; some of these appear to be involved in giving false teaching.
7 Look closely in Genesis 3:6; the text clearly says that Adam was 'with her' at the time! Indeed, this makes them equally culpable.
8 Genesis 3:6-7.
9 Genesis 3:8.
10 Genesis 3:9-10.
11 Genesis 3:24-25.

What's God Up To…?

12 Some feel that the Bible is not true at this point for God had said that if they ate of the fruit they would surely die (Genesis 2:17). Yet in reality, death is a process in which we decay and death overwhelms life to the point at which we expire. This process was kicked off at that moment, and since that day, to live ultimately means to die. Some argue death existed before this point. While this is possible, Romans 5:12 makes it unlikely.
13 Genesis 3:11.
14 Genesis 3:12.
15 Genesis 3:13-14.
16 Genesis 3:14-15. Some take this literally. However, the symbolism of the snake (= Satan) suggests this probably means that Satan would spend his days on earth contending with humanity, seeking to destroy them. The text also predicts a day when a human (Jesus) will rise up and destroy Satan (Genesis 3:15).
17 Genesis 3:16.
18 Genesis 3:19.
19 See Romans 8:19-22 which speaks of the whole of creation desperately and eagerly waiting for its release from bondage to corruption, decay and death.
20 As it is described in Genesis 1:31.
21 Some Christians hold that death existed in the animal world before the Fall. They see the Fossils as evidence of this. They hold to a view of evolutionary theism or theistic evolution. The Fall separated humanity from the source of eternal life (tree of life), and sin and death entered *human* experience. Others maintain death entered at this point.
22 You can read about this story in 2 Samuel 11-12.
23 Psalms 51:5.
24 1 Kings 8:46.
25 Mark 10:18.
26 Romans 3:9, 10, 12, 23.
27 Romans 5:12.
28 See Romans 8:19-23.
29 See Genesis 1:31.
30 Check out 1 Peter 5:8 where the devil is described as a prowling lion looking for someone to devour. Or look at John 10:10 where he is described as 'a thief' who comes to 'steal, kill and destroy'. Paul also warns believers not to give him a foothold (Ephesians 4:27).
31 This should not be misunderstood to imply that individual sin directly leads to these problems. Rather, the whole cosmic problem of evil plays out in these specific problems and others.
32 Matthew 4:9.
33 See John 10:10 where the 'thief' is a description of Satan.

34 Matthew 5:28.
35 This is a truth we see on the news. Our jails are full of people who are in fact victims of horrendous treatment and abuse. What this indicates is that the image of God in these people is more broken than in others. They have been violated in their humanity by others.
36 Check out the whole Sermon on the Mount (Matthew 5-7; Luke 6:17-49); other lists of vices (e.g. Matthew 15:17-20; Mark 7:21-23; Romans 1:28-32; 1 Corinthians 6:9-10; 2 Corinthians 12:20; Galatians 5:19-22) and passages where Paul outlines the ideals of Christian behaviour (esp. Romans 12; Galatians 4-6; Ephesians 4:17-6:20; Colossians 3-4).
37 Romans 7:18-19: 'For I have the desire to do what is good, but I cannot carry it out. For what I do is not the good I want to do; no, the evil I do not want to do—this I keep on doing.'
38 Galatians 3:22.
39 Romans 3:23.
40 Apart from Jesus (see below).
41 Galatians 3:22.
42 Romans 6:23.
43 Jesus: Matthew 5:22, 29-30; 18:9; 25:41 ('the eternal fire prepared for the devil and his angels'). Paul: Galatians 6:8; Philippians 3:19; 2 Thessalonians 1:9 ('everlasting destruction'); Jude 7; John in Revelation 20:12-15.
44 See Matthew 24:4-31 for example.
45 This is seen in verses which emphasise God's love for us even though we are sinful people; for example Romans 5:6, 8. See also Romans 8:35, 39: 'nothing in all creation can separate us from the love of God.' We are loved despite our propensity to sin.
46 This is the concept of foreknowledge and predestination. God is outside time. He knows all future eventualities. At the moment of creation he knew all that would happen, it was predestined. However, this did not mean that there was no volition within history as it played out. While all eventualities were foreknown and predestined, as human existence is lived out, we have the ability to choose God's way or our own way. On this basis we will be judged.

Chapter 3: Restoration

1 One could equally call this reconciliation or redemption.
2 Most Christians accept a literal flood, but differ as to whether it covered the whole world, or the known world. Some see it as a metaphorical event symbolic of God's recreation.
3 Genesis 6:5.

What's God Up To…?

4 Luke 19:41.
5 Ephesians 4:30.
6 John 3:16.
7 Romans 5:8.
8 1 John 4:8.
9 Psalms 136:1.
10 1 Timothy 1:1; 2:3; 4:10.
11 Genesis 3:21.
12 Genesis 6-9.
13 Genesis 11.
14 Genesis 12:1-3; 15; 17.
15 Genesis 37-50.
16 Exodus 3-14.
17 Numbers.
18 The so-called 'Ten Commandments' (Exodus 20:1-17; 5:1-22).
19 Joshua.
20 1 Samuel-Malachi.
21 Some verses which Christians believe refer to the Messiah from the line of David include Deuteronomy 7:9-16; 1 Chronicles 17:1-14; Psalms 2; 18:50; 89; 110; Isaiah 9:2-7; 11:1-5; Jeremiah 23:5-6; 33:17-18; Ezekiel 34:33-34; 37:24-28; Amos 9:11-15; Zechariah 12:7-13:1. See also Zechariah 9:9. There are texts which Israel did not recognise as referring to the Messiah, the so-called Servant Songs of Isaiah which tell of a suffering Messiah (Isaiah 42:1-6; 49:1-7; 50:4-11; 52:13-53:12; 61:1-2. See also Psalms 22).
22 To understand this requires reading the book of Leviticus with all its rituals and regulations. Also read the book of Hebrews and Acts 7, 13 which give great insight into how to understand the Old Testament in light of the coming of Christ.
23 Read the account in Genesis 22. It seems astonishing that God would ask a man to sacrifice his son. However, God never intended that Abraham would kill Isaac; rather, he sent the ram as a replacement to save him. The ram is in a sense a 'prototype' of Jesus, the Lamb of God sent to take away the sins of the world (John 1:29).
24 See John 2:19-21 where the resurrected *Jesus* is the temple; 1 Corinthians 3:16 where *the church* is now the temple, not a building, but a people; 1 Corinthians 6:19 where *individually* we are the temple of God who dwells in us. See also Ephesians 2:19-22. Note that the church properly understood is not a building, but a people i.e. the people of God who believe in Jesus as Saviour and Lord.
25 Hebrews 7.
26 1 Corinthians 5:7; John 1:29. See Exodus 12 for the story of Passover.
27 Romans 3:20; Galatians 3:24. Read Exodus 19-20 for the original account of the giving of the Law.

Notes

28 In Bethlehem (800 yrs prior [Micah 5:2; Matthew 2:6]); of a virgin (800 years prior [Isaiah 7:14; Matthew 1:23]); his flight to Egypt (800 years before [Hosea 11:1; Matthew 2:15]); the slaughter of innocent children (600 years before [Jeremiah 31:15; Matthew 2:18]); that it would be preceded by a prophet like Elijah, John the Baptist ([Isaiah 40:3; Matthew 3:3]).

29 Galilee (Isaiah 9:1-2; Matthew 4:14-16).

30 Isaiah 29:18; 35:5-6; 42:7; Matthew 11:4-5.

31 Jesus is the fulfilment of the expected servant of Isaiah (Isaiah 42:1-7; 49:1-6; 50:4-9; 52:13-53:12). In the latter text his suffering is explicitly referred to. Similarly the suffering and death of the Messiah is predicted with amazing detail in Psalms 22 including asphyxiation and the casting of lots for his clothing.

32 See Psalms 16:8-10; Hosea 6:2; and the 'sign of Jonah' who spent 3 days and nights in the belly of a fish (see Jonah 1-2; Matthew 12:39-40; 16:4).

33 See Matthew 1:20-25; Luke 1:28-35.

34 See John 1:1, 14: 'In the beginning was the Word (Jesus) and the *Word was God* ... the Word became flesh and made his dwelling among us.'

35 See Mark 12:29-31. See also the so-called 'Golden Rule': so in everything, do to others what you would have them do for you' (Matthew 7:12).

36 Matthew 5-7. See also Luke's version, 'The Sermon on the Plain' in Luke 6.

37 See Mark 10:39-45. In this passage Jesus declares that he came to serve and not to be served (as one might expect of a king). He tells the disciples that they are to lead by being servants and give their lives for others refusing to use power, military might, status or rank as a means of domination. All Christians are to do the same.

38 Read John 6:15 where the crowds who have just witnessed an astonishing miracle want to make him king by force. Jesus refuses.

39 See Mark 8:27-38. They confess him as Messiah and he immediately turns their attention to the nature of being a Messiah. He will suffer and die.

40 See Matthew 16:24; Mark 8:34; Luke 9:23; 14:27.

41 An astonishing response from the cross: 'Father, forgive them, for they do not know what they are doing' (Luke 23:34).

42 Have a read of Philippians 2:6-11 where Paul sings of Jesus that he was God, but became a man, a servant, died on a cross, and was raised to be exalted as Lord of the universe... this is the way of God, service.

43 This does not mean God died. He was killed but God the Father, Spirit and Christ (spiritually), continued to exist. Such a thought led to intense discussions in the christological debates of the early church. What is clear is that Jesus was genuinely killed, but God did not die! Where Jesus then went is debated. Some believe he descended to hell (check out 1 Peter 3:19; 4:6). Others believe he went directly to heaven (check out Luke 23:43: '*today* you will be with me in paradise').

44 Read here 1 Corinthians 15:12-19 where Paul points out the consequences of

there being no bodily resurrection including: a. Christian preaching is pointless; b. Christian faith is meaningless; c. The first Christians were false-witnesses; d. All humanity is still separated from God and destined for eternal separation; e. Those Christians who have died are separated from God; f. Christians are to be pitied more than any other people.

45   One of the most astonishing aspects of the accounts is the retention of Mary Magdalene as the first witness of the resurrection. A woman's testimony was considered worthless, yet the first Christians retained this element in the account.

46   Read Matthew 27:57-28:20; Mark 16:1-20; Luke 24; John 20-21; Acts 1:1-11; 1 Corinthians 15 esp. vs 1-11. Each passage records that Jesus died, that he was entombed, that there was an empty tomb and that there were multiple appearances of Jesus. Christians disagree on the number of appearances due to the differences in detail. Some reject these accounts on the detail differences. Another view I hold is that these differences actually indicate the honesty and integrity of the accounts and rule out collusion by the first Christians. In addition, these witnesses were almost all martyred for their view, without any financial or other gain… why would they do so unless their accounts are not authentic? This supports the authenticity of the resurrection.

47   For example Stephen in Acts 7; James in Acts 12:1; Peter and Paul under Nero in AD 64-68. Tradition has it that all but John were put to death. Why would good people die for a lie for no material, or other, gain?

48   Other theories fail. The body could not have been stolen because of the guard and the rock. Jesus could not have been merely asleep because he was clearly dead, was severely beaten, had his side pierced by a spear, could not have moved the stone and eluded the guards. The women could not have gone to the wrong tomb as they were with Joseph of Arimathea (the owner of the tomb) when Jesus was buried. Similarly, hallucination explanations are unlikely in that they occurred across a range of times, huge geographical range, involved large groups seeing him simultaneously (see John 21; 1 Corinthians 15; Matthew 28:16-20) and the disciples had no expectation of the event.

49   Acts 1:11. Christians differ as to whether this event was a literal rising up into the clouds or a figurative departure. I think it is most likely the former as the return of Christ is said to be Jesus returning in the same way from heaven.

50   Check out again Philippians 2:6-11; a hymn or poem speaking of how Jesus though God, emptied himself of his prerogatives as God the Son, became human and a slave, was totally obedient to death, and so rose to be exalted to the right hand of God as Lord of all. All humanity will one day bow before him either voluntarily or involuntarily. His desire is that it is voluntary and we live with him forever.

51   Hebrews 4:15: 'he was without sin' cf. 2 Corinthians 5:21.

52   Romans 5:12: 'Therefore, just as sin entered the world through one man, and death

Notes

through sin, and in this way death came to all people, because all sinned.' Romans 6:23: 'for the wages of sin is death.'

53 For example Leviticus 17:11: 'I have given it to you to make *atonement* for yourselves on the altar; it is the blood that makes atonement for one's life.'

54 Another term used by some scholars is 'propitiation' which means the removal of God's wrath by the offering of a gift (i.e. Jesus death averts the wrath of God).

55 Romans 3:23-24: 'For all have sinned and fall short of the glory of God, and are *justified* freely by his grace through the redemption that came by Christ Jesus.'

56 So Paul can say we are 'children of God' and not slaves (see Galatians 4:6). So John can say we are 'friends' of God (John 14:13-15).

57 Romans 5:8-11: 'But God demonstrates his own love for us in this: While we were still sinners, Christ died for us. Since we have now been *justified* by his blood, how much more shall we be *saved* from God's wrath through him! For if, when *we were God's enemies*, we were *reconciled* to him through the death of his Son, how much more, having been reconciled, shall we be saved through his life!'

58 See Colossians 1:20 where Paul writes of God reconciling all things to Christ. This is the purpose of God, to restore his world.

59 1 Corinthians 1:30: 'It is because of him that you are in Christ Jesus, who has become for us wisdom from God – that is, our righteousness, *holiness* and redemption.' Another way of saying this is by calling Christians 'holy ones' or 'saints' e.g. 1 Corinthians 1:2.

60 The process of becoming more holy is called 'sanctification.' Fully understood, 'sanctification' is a status we receive at the point of faith. We are to continue to live this out becoming better and better people.

61 Romans 8:15: 'For you did not receive a spirit that makes you a slave again to fear, but you received the Spirit of *adoption*. And by him we cry, *"Abba*, Father."' See also John 1:12-13: 'Yet to all who received him, to those who believed in his name, he gave the right to become children of God – children born not of natural descent, nor of human decision or a husband's will, but born of God.' See also Galatians 4:6.

62 Romans 8:17: 'Now if we are children, then we are heirs – heirs of God and co-heirs with Christ.'

63 See Romans 8: 17: '… if indeed we share in his sufferings in order that we may also share in his glory.'

64 John 1:12: 'Yet to all who received him, to those who believed in his name, he gave the right to become children of God – children born not of natural descent, nor of human decision or a husband's will, but born of God.'

65 See John 3:3, 5: 'Jesus declared, 'I tell you the truth, no one can see the kingdom of God unless he is born again." Nicodemus did not fully understand, thinking Jesus meant to re-enter a mother's womb again! Jesus clarified: 'I tell you the truth, no one can enter the kingdom of God unless he is born of water and the

Spirit.' Scholars argue about the meaning of this. 'Water and Spirit' here may be synonyms, or 'water' may refer to baptism or to natural birth.
66   See Titus 3:5.
67   Romans 6:4: 'We were therefore *buried with him* through baptism into *death* in order that, just as Christ was *raised* from the dead through the glory of the Father, we too may live a new life.'
68   Ephesians 2:1: 'As for you, you were dead in your transgressions and sins.'
69   See Romans 5:12; 1 Corinthians 15:22, 45.
70   Galatians 2:20: 'I have been crucified with Christ and I no longer live, but Christ lives in me.'
71   John 3:3 above.
72   Ephesians 1:7: 'In him we have redemption through his blood.'
73   Romans 8:1: 'There is no guilt for those in Christ Jesus.'
74   Ephesians 1:7: 'In him... the forgiveness of sin.'
75   Luke 19:10.
76   Romans 8:24: 'For in this hope we *were* saved.'
77   1 Corinthians 1:18: 'For the message of the cross is foolishness to those who are perishing, but to us who *are being* saved it is the power of God.'
78   Romans 10:9: 'That you confess with your mouth, 'Jesus is Lord,' and believe in your heart that God raised him from the dead, you *will be* saved.'
79   Genesis 4.
80   Genesis 5-9.
81   Genesis 10-11.
82   On Jesus as sinless see 2 Corinthians 5:21; Hebrews 4:15.
83   See Luke 19:10.
84   See Luke 5:27-32.
85   See Mark 12:31; Luke 10:27; Romans 13:9; Galatians 5:14 (the summary of all law); James 2:8 (the 'royal law'). See also John 13:34-35; Matthew 7:12 ('do to others, as you would have them do to you' i.e. the 'Golden Rule' which summarises all OT writings). See also Matthew 5:44; 6:27, 35 where this love is not just for our loved ones and those who will return our love, but it is love even for our enemies. Imagine a world where this was lived out... that is the eternity that awaits us. See also 1 John 3:16-17 too where true love is found in the love of Christ for us, giving up his life for us, and involves sacrifice for those in need. See also 1 Corinthians 13 and 1 John 4.
86   See Luke 6:27. Read the whole section to verse 36. What an astonishing ethic! Jesus commands his followers to love those who hate them including invading forces!
87   See 1 John 3:16-17; Ephesians 5:1-2.
88   Romans 5:8.
89   See John 15:13.

Notes

90 See John 3:16: note that this love is not just for humanity, but for all of humanity and the whole natural world.
91 See Acts 2:1-4; 2 Corinthians 1:21-22; Ephesians 1:13-14.
92 See Galatians 5:22-23. Just as a tree bears fruit, as we respond to the Spirit within, we will bear the attributes of love, joy, peace, patience, kindness, goodness, faithfulness, gentleness and self-control. See also 1 Corinthians 13.
93 See Galatians 3:28: 'there is neither Jew nor Greek, slave nor free, male nor female, for you are all one in Christ Jesus.'
94 Look through these references to the Kingdom of God in Jesus' teaching in particular: Matthew 4:17, 23; 6:33; 9:35; 12:28; 13:24, 31, 33, 44, 45; 18:3-4; 19:23-24; 24:14; 25:34; Luke 4:43; 9:62; 10:9, 11; 17:21; 18:29; John 3:3, 5. Matthew most often uses the phrase 'Kingdom of Heaven' which is a parallel phrase.
95 Mark 1:14.
96 Some translate this as 'within you' referring to the inward subjective experience of the Kingdom within the human heart. However, it is more likely that this should be translated 'among you', meaning that in the presence of the listeners is the Kingdom in the person of Jesus.
97 Check out John 1:1-18. Here Jesus is God the Word who created the world (1:1-2), who came to his own world as a part of it ('flesh'), to save it. It is such an amazing idea – God the creator, becomes a creature, to save his world, all creatures and especially humanity.
98 There is a long history of debate concerning 'when' the Kingdom comes. Some scholars argue that Jesus spoke of it coming completely in his time (a 'realised view of the Kingdom'). Others see it completely as future (a 'futuristic view'). Others like myself take it in an inaugurated sense – i.e. the Kingdom has come, established in the person and ministry of Jesus the King. It will grow in the context of human history through the work of the Holy Spirit in the world and through God's people and, at some future unknown point in history, Jesus will return and the Kingdom will be culminated.
99 Matthew 13:31-32.
100 Matthew 13:33.
101 Matthew 5:13.
102 John 8:12.
103 Matthew 5:16; see also Philippians 2:14-15.
104 Interestingly, this parable is now being realised. According to www.adherents.com/Religions_By_Adherents.html (24 Oct, 2009) Christianity has 2.1b adherents (33%). Other faiths/ideologies include Islam (1.5 b = 21%); Secular/nonreligious/agnostic/atheist (1.1b = 16%); Hinduism (900m = 14%); Chinese Traditional (394m = 6%); Buddhism (376m = 6%); Primal-indigenous (300m = 6%); Sikh (23m = 0.4%); Judaism (14m = 0.2%); Bahai (7m = 0.1%).

105 Peter, Andrew, James and John were fishermen. Levi was a tax-collector. Simon was a Zealot, a mercenary who longed to overthrow the Romans (see Luke 6:13).
106 See Luke 8:1-4 where those who travelled with him included Mary Magdalene who had been dreadfully demonised, Johanna who was the wife of the manager of King Herod's household and others. Incidentally, contrary to popular thinking, there is no direct evidence in the New Testament that Mary Magdalene was a prostitute.
107 2 Corinthians 5:21: 'God made him who had no sin to be sin for us, so that in him we might become the righteousness of God.'

Chapter 4: Return

1 This is part of what some call an apocalyptic schema. An apocalyptic perspective dominates the NT in the teaching of Jesus and Paul in particular. History is interpreted against the backdrop of a fallen, dark evil world. God will intervene with his salvation to free his people, end the dominance of evil and establish his reign.
2 One example is Mark 10:29-30 where Jesus says to the disciples, 'no one who has left home... will fail to receive a hundred times as much *in this present age* ... and *in the age to come*, eternal life.' See also Matthew 12:32; 13:39, 40, 49; 24:3; 28:20; Ephesians 1:21 among many others.
3 Galatians 1:13; 2 Corinthians 4:4.
4 Acts 1:11.
5 Mark 13:26. See also Matthew 24:30; Luke 24:27. This recalls and will fulfil the prophecy of Daniel of such an event some 600 years before Christ (Daniel 7:13-14).
6 1 Thessalonians 4:16.
7 This means Jesus is placed in a position of supremacy over the universe. It fulfils the prediction of Psalms 110:1: 'The Lord said to my Lord: "Sit at my right hand until I make your enemies a footstool for your feet." Paul tells us that this will be completed at the culmination of history (see 1 Corinthians 15:20-24).
8 Acts 2:33. Note that this is a fulfilment of the prophecy of Joel that the Spirit will pour out in the last days on humanity (see Acts 2:17-21; Joel 2:28-32).
9 Philippians 2:9. Here Paul is referring to Isaiah 45:23; where Jesus will fulfil on his return the prediction of Isaiah 800 years before Christ that all will bow in this way.
10 See earlier in Philippians 2:6 where it is written: 'who (Christ Jesus), being *in very nature God*... but he emptied himself.' Check out Romans 9:5 too where Paul writes that the 'Messiah (Jesus), is God over all!' See also John 1:1 ('the Word was God'), Colossians 1:15 ('He is the image of the invisible God') and Hebrews 1:1 ('The Son is the radiance of God's glory and the exact representation of his being, sustaining all things by his powerful word').

Notes

11 G.F. Zeolla notes (see www.dtl.org/dtl/treatise/end-near-1.htm [Sept, 2007]) that 'on new year's eve, 1000 AD, a crowd gathered at Rome, awaiting the end of the world. Midnight came, nothing happened and the pope, Sylvester II, blessed the crowd and sent them home.' Similarly, 'In the expectation of the approaching judgment, crowds of pilgrims flocked to Palestine to greet the advent of the Savior. But the first millennium passed, and Christendom awoke with a sigh of relief on the first day of the year 1001.'

12 See http://en.wikipedia.org/wiki/Criticism_of_Jehovah's_Witnesses (Oct, 2009).

13 See H. Lindsay, *The Late Great Planet Earth* (Grand Rapids: Zondervan, 1970); S. Swihart, *Armageddon 198?* (Plainfield: Haven Books, 1980).

14 Matthew 24:36.

15 Matthew 24:37-41.

16 In this section I have not discussed more difficult and controversial signs from the Old Testament and the apocalyptic Book of Revelation. While I believe these give details to us concerning the end, discerning them is much more complicated and Christians are far from agreement about them. Hence, I have only referred to those in the Gospels and the writings of Paul which are less unambiguous. Some Christians do not think these passages are about the return of Christ at all. So, while all Bible-believing Christians believe that Jesus will ultimately return, there is great diversity of views about exactly what will precede this event, how and when it will happen.

17 Matthew 24:32.

18 See for what follows the three parallel passages in Mark 13; Matthew 24; Luke 21. These passages are called the 'Olivet Discourse' or 'little apocalypse' by some. Some think they relate only to the Fall of Jerusalem in A.D. 70. Others, like myself, believe they refer to both events, the Fall of Jerusalem and the return of Christ.

19 Matthew 24:4-8; Mark 13:5-8; Luke 21:8-10.

20 See for example W. Pratney, B. Chant, *The Return* (Sovereign World, 1989). They note in the 16th C = 153; 17th C = 378; 18th C = 640; 19th C = 119; 20th C = more than all history together). However, others suggest this is inaccurate e.g. See also http://earth.webecs.co.uk/index.htm (Sept, 2007). But see www.icr.org/research/index/researchp_sa_r06/ (Sept 2007) which argues the converse.

21 Mark 13:10: 'And the gospel must first be preached to *all nations*;' Matthew 24:14: 'and this gospel of the kingdom will be preached *in the whole world* as a testimony *to all nations*, and then the end will come.' Note that some Christians believe that this does not indicate the proclamation of the gospel to all nations in an empirical sense, but that it simply means that the gospel will be preached in the period after Christ's resurrection throughout the world.

22 This is called the 'Great Commission.' Jesus commanded his disciples to go to all the world to preach the good news so that people would believe in him and experience relationship with God and the world restored. See Matthew 28:18-20; Luke 24:46-49; John 20:21; Acts 1:8 cf. Mark 16:15-20.

23   See Romans 15:19-33.
24   The best example is Ephesus which was the key city in the province of Asia Minor. Paul planted a church there and from his base there, the whole of Asia heard the message within a two year period (Acts 19:9-10). You can also check this principle out in 1 Thessalonians 1:6-8; Acts 13:48-49.
25   See www.joshuaproject.net/index.php (sighted, 10 April, 2009).
26   See Matthew 24:15; Mark 13:14-15; 2 Thessalonians 2.
27   See 2 Thessalonians 2.
28   Mark 13:12-13; Luke 21:12-19.
29   Mark 13:12-13; Luke 21:12-19.
30   Matthew 24:24-28; Mark 13:21-22.
31   Matthew 24:29; Mark 13:24-25. Note that some Christians read these as apocalyptic symbolism and that they should not be seen as literal.
32   Luke 24:20.
33   The majority of scholars believe that Mark's Gospel was written in the early to mid 60s AD around the time of the apostle Peter's death. See 'Gospel of Mark,' in Joel B. Green, Scot McKnight, I. H. Marshall, *Dictionary of Jesus and the Gospels* (Downers Grove: IVP, 1992), 514.
34   The first exile occurred in the northern tribes of Israel when the Assyrians invaded and exiled many (721 BC). The second occurred when the Babylonians invaded Judah and Jerusalem and exiled many (587 BC). This lasted some 70 years when Babylon fell and many returned to Jerusalem.
35   See for example Zechariah 12.
36   Luke 24:32.
37   The signs are listed in Luke 21:25-28.
38   Luke 21:27.
39   1 Thessalonians 4:16. These may be literal or figurative indicating an enormous cosmic event.
40   Matthew 24:40-41.
41   1 Thessalonians 4:16-17.
42   Postmillenialists are very positive about God's work in history, believing the world will gradually be Christianised and improve and God's reign will be seen through the whole world, and then Christ will come. Amillenialists agree that the period of the church is the millennium, but believe that the world will deteriorate and come to a dramatic climax at the return of Christ.
43   Whichever is the correct view is made very difficult because of the symbolism in Revelation which leaves interpretation uncertain along with dispute over what is meant by: 1) The binding of the devil? 2) the meaning of the 1000 years? 3) Satan's release? 4) The people who come to life? 5) The first resurrection, physical or spiritual? 6) Reigning with Christ for 1000 years? There are various possibilities and

complex arguments supporting each. It is better to allow diversity of opinion and resist dogmatism on these things, majoring on the things that are clear.

44 For example 1 Thessalonians 4:16; Hebrews 9:27.
45 For example Matthew 25:31-46 (judgement for care of needy). See also Matthew 12:36-37 (judgement for speech); John 5:22 (Jesus the judge); Romans 2:5; 14:10-11; 2 Corinthians 5:10; Hebrews 6:2; 10:27; 2 Peter 2:9.
46 This does not mean people are saved by being good or following a religious system other than Christianity. Rather, they are saved because they perceived God and walked in relationship with him *by faith*. The best example of this in the Bible is Abraham, who Paul tells us was saved on the basis of his faith *before Jesus came to earth*. Another example is Melchezidek in Hebrews 7 and the list of people 'of faith' in Hebrews 11. Paul also considers those who do not recognise God through creation as 'without excuse' because he is there to be seen by his handiwork (see Romans 1:20).
47 Revelation 21:1-4; 2 Peter 3:13.
48 For example: for a renewed earth see Romans 8:19-22; for a new creation see 2 Peter 3:10; Revelation 21:1-4.
49 See Matthew 25:34: 'Then the King will say to those on his right, "Come, you who are blessed by my Father; take your inheritance, the kingdom prepared for you since the creation of the world."' See also Revelation 21:1-4: 'Then I saw a new heaven and a new earth, for the first heaven and the first earth had passed away, and there was no longer any sea. I saw the Holy City, the new Jerusalem, coming down out of heaven from God, prepared as a bride beautifully dressed for her husband. And I heard a loud voice from the throne saying, "Now the dwelling of God is with humanity, and he will live with them. They will be his people, and God himself will be with them and be their God. He will wipe every tear from their eyes. There will be no more death or mourning or crying or pain, for the old order of things has passed away."'
50 See for example: Matthew 9:43-45; 25:41, 46; 2 Thessalonians 1:6-10; Revelation 20:14-15.
51 This is the view I prefer.
52 Called 'conditional immortality' whereby only those who are saved become immortal, the others are annihilated.
53 Matthew 24:42.
54 Matthew 24:45-51. The Parable of the Ten Virgins.
55 Matthew 25:14-30: The Parable of the Talents.
56 Matthew 25:31-46: The account of the Sheep and the Goats.

Chapter 5: Response

1. Acts 16:31.
2. See 1 Timothy 2:4: 'who (God) wants *all men and women* to be saved and to come to a knowledge of the truth.' See also 2 Peter 3:9: 'He (God) is patient with you, not wanting *anyone* to perish, but *everyone* to come to repentance.'
3. For example Matthew 25:41; Philippians 1:28; Revelation 21:15. The fact that not all will be saved rules out the idea of *universalism* i.e. that all will be ultimately saved no matter what their response. Potentially all can be saved through Jesus (potential universalism). Actually, not all will be (e.g. Luke 13:24-30).
4. Matthew 4:17; Mark 1:15.
5. Matthew 11:20-21; Luke 13:3, 5.
6. Luke 5:32.
7. Mark 6:12; Luke 24:47 cf. Luke 13:3, 5. Jesus also said then when a person does repent, God and his angels have a party to celebrate in heaven (Luke 15:7, 10)! This is because the original relationship God intended with that person is restored!
8. Louw and Nida, *Greek-English Lexicon of the New Testament Based on Semantic Domains*. 2nd Edition. Vol 1 (New York: UBS, 1988, 89), 41.52.
9. Matthew 4:19.
10. Matthew 9:9.
11. Matthew 19:21.
12. Matthew 6:33.
13. Luke 9:23.
14. Luke 9:24-25.
15. Matthew 7:12-13.
16. Matthew 24:13.
17. See Romans 8:28.
18. John 1:12-13.
19. John 3:36. See also John 5:24: 'I tell you the truth, whoever hears my word and believes in him who sent me has eternal life and will not be condemned; he has crossed over from death to life.'
20. Romans 3:22.
21. Ephesians 2:8.
22. Some think faith here is the gift from God meaning we do not have a say in our own believing; rather, God grants some to believe and some not to by his grace. This is not correct grammatically as the gender of the Greek word for 'gift' here suggests the whole clause is in mind with 'this' i.e. the salvation is the gift of God.
23. Ephesians 1:13-14.
24. Romans 10:17.
25. I say 'usually' because sometimes God intervenes directly through personal

26 The Parable of the Sower speaks of the message being like a seed planted in the human heart. For some it leads to fruitful faith. For others it does not (read Mark 4:1-20).
27 Ephesians 2:8-9.
28 Paul says as much in 2 Corinthians 5:14: 'For the love of Christ compels us, having been convinced of this, that Christ died for all.'
29 Have a read here of Paul's argument in Romans 6. He counters the idea that God's grace is such that we can go on sinning. 'No way!' he says. Out of gratitude for the grace and mercy of God, we will seek to serve him and live righteously.
30 Ephesians 2:10.
31 Check out Romans 4 for this.
32 Romans 4:2 cf. Genesis 15:6.
33 For these you can check out Genesis 12:10-20; 16:1-16; 20:1-17.
34 See Romans 4:16-23.
35 While all of us will receive at least one such spiritual gift, no individual receives every gift. Rather, God distributes the gifts throughout his people and we must work together in humility, love and harmony with these gifts to further God's work in the world. All gifts are of equal importance despite some appearing more impressive and desirable. If you want to know more read these passages on spiritual gifts: Romans 12:3-8; 1 Corinthians 12-14; Ephesians 4:11-16.
36 Philippians 1:6.

Chapter 6: Where to from Here?

1 See Luke 15:7,10
2 See Hebrews 13:5,6; Matthew 28:20
3 Matthew 6:9-13. There are different versions. Try this one: 'Our Father in heaven, holy is your character and being. May your reign be established. May your purposes be done on earth as it is in heaven. Please give us this day the food we need. Please forgive us our sins, as we forgive those who sin against us. And please do not bring us into times of testing, but rescue us from evil. For the Kingdom, the power and the glory is yours forever and ever, Amen.'
4 Check out the story of Peter's denial of Jesus and his restoration. He denied Jesus but Jesus restored him and he became the leader of the church. Read John 13:36-38; 18:15-18 and the whole of John 21. Then read Acts 1-8 and see Peter the leaders. Read too Peter's letters, 1 and 2 Peter! What a great story!
5 Have a read of the story of the thief on the cross. As he hung on the cross waiting to

die he heard Jesus say, 'Father forgive them, for they do not know what they do' and he realised that Jesus was the King of Israel and the world. So he acknowledged Jesus. Jesus responded by telling him that on this day ('today') he would be with Jesus in paradise! That is, he would spend eternity with God. Read Luke 23:34-43.

6   See Hebrews 10:25: 'Do not give up the habit of meeting together.' See also Acts 2:44-46.

7   The ancient Jews met on the Sabbath (Friday evening to Saturday). The early Christians began in this way and shifted to gathering on the day of the resurrection, the Sunday – the first day of the week (See Matthew 28:1; Acts 20:7; 1 Corinthians 16:2).

8   The original Greek *baptizō* means to 'wash, dip, immerse' and was also used as a metaphor for dying.

9   To understand baptism further read these verses: Matthew 3:6-16; 28:18-20; John 3:22-23; 4:1-2; Acts 2:38-41; 8:12, 36; 10:47-48; 16:15, 33; 18:8; Romans 6:3-4; Galatians 3:26-29. Some churches baptise infants (infant baptism or christening). Others do not as they believe that only people capable of independent belief can be baptised. This is not the sort of issue that should divide us. Talk to your church leaders about this and do what Peter says in Acts 2:38: 'Repent and be baptised'.

10   To understand the Lord's Supper read these verses: Matthew 26:17-30; Mark 14:12-26; Luke 22:7-38; John 13:1-38; Acts 2:42-47 (note the phrase 'breaking of bread', this means eating a meal and celebrating the Lord's Supper); 1 Corinthians 11:17-33. Baptism and the Lord's Supper are also called sacraments (sacred occasion).

11   Check out 2 Peter 1:5-8.

12   Take for example Romans 12:2 and Philippians 4:8.

13   See 1 Corinthians 10:26 which is a quote from Psalms 24:1.

14   Check out the stories in Luke 15. Each talks about what happens when a person says yes to Jesus. In each, God has a party! That is how happy he is when we turn to him because that is his intention i.e. for everyone to live forever with God (see chapter one).

15   Mark 2:13-17.

16   See 1 Corinthians 7:17-24.

17   See 1 Corinthians 7:12-16.

18   See 1 Corinthians 10:24-30; 14:20-25.

19   See 1 Corinthians 9:3-23; 1 Thessalonians 2; 2 Thessalonians 3:7-12.

20   See Ephesians 4:28; 1 Thessalonians 4:11-12; Colossians 3:23.

Appendix 1: Am I Really a Sinner?

1   See Deuteronomy 6:5; Leviticus 19:18.

ABOUT THE AUTHOR

Mark Keown is a New Zealander living in Auckland. He is married to Emma, a Presbyterian Minister, and has three daughters. He was not raised in an active Christian family, but became a devoted follower of Jesus in his early twenties.

He is a lover of sport having been involved in cricket, rugby and indoor rowing to competitive levels.

He has a doctorate, from the Australian College of Theology, on evangelism in Paul's letter to the Philippians. Aside from a number of articles, this is his second work, the other being a technical study, *Congregational Evangelism in Philippians* (Milton Keynes: Paternoster, 2008). He is currently working on a commentary on Philippians to be completed in 2011 in the Exegetical Expositional Series.

Mark currently teaches at Laidlaw College (formerly Bible College of New Zealand) specialising in New Testament studies. He is often found preaching in churches, camps and anywhere anyone wants to hear about Jesus. He can be found on Facebook and his blog is http://drmarkk.blogspot.com/.

www.ingramcontent.com/pod-product-compliance
Lightning Source LLC
Chambersburg PA
CBHW060822190426
43197CB00038B/2195